Led by the
SPIRIT

How God Guides
and Provides

BILLY JOE
DAUGH

CREATION
HOUSE
BOOKS ABOUT SPIRIT-LED LIVING
ORLANDO, FLORIDA

Creation House
Strang Communications Company
600 Rinehart Road
Lake Mary, FL 32746
Phone: 407-333-3132
Fax: 407-333-7100
Web site: http://www.strang.com

First printing, November 1994
Second printing, April 1995
Third printing, July 1995
Fourth printing, November 1996

To my Lord and Savior, Jesus Christ,
who sent the Holy Spirit
to lead us into all truth

CONTENTS

PREFACE

One of the best memories of my dad happened during a seventh-grade track meet. I was running the 440-yard dash, which is one lap around the track.

At the start of the race, my dad was in the bleachers watching with the other parents and students. The gun sounded and the race was on. My speed was about average, putting me in the middle of the group of runners.

As we rounded the last curve and headed down

the stretch toward the finish line, I heard my dad's voice yelling, "Come on, Billy Joe, come on!" I looked to my left on the infield of the track and there was my dad running right with me, yelling every step of the way. He had left the bleachers and gotten into the race with me.

Over the years I've reflected how Jesus was sent to join us in the race. With every step, He's shouting, "Come on, you can do it!" He wants us to win more than we do.

As you read this book, it is my prayer that you will see the Holy Spirit in the race with you, cheering you on to victory!

CHAPTER ONE

LED BY THE SPIRIT

When I was in my twenties, I had the wonderful experience of staying at a boarding house run by an opinionated 87-year-old bundle of energy called Mrs. Davis.

One day I was in my room when I heard a knock at the front door. Mrs. Davis answered it, and I overheard just a few words. A man's voice was saying, "Ma'am, I've got some books here that I would like to share with you." Then I heard the door slam shut. Mrs. Davis didn't give him the time of day — she just slammed the door right in his face.

Something inside of me said, "Go out there and see who that was."

I went to the door, opened it and saw the guy still standing there holding a book. He had an awful look of disappointment on his face, as if to say, "You know, this is the thirtieth time today...." He explained he was traveling that summer trying to raise some money selling encyclopedias. I don't know if you have ever tried doing that, but it's tough!

I invited him to sit down on the porch swing so we could talk. I shared with him about the Lord, and I had an opportunity to pray with him to commit his life to Jesus Christ.

I've thought back on that experience and how just a little voice inside my spirit said, "Go out there and speak to him." The Holy Spirit led me to talk with that young man because God had already prepared his heart to receive Christ.

God used that experience in my life to teach me what it means to be led by the Spirit. Through my life it's been a step-by-step process of learning to listen, following His guidance and seeing His provision.

There's a passage in Romans that sums up the most important facts about being led by the Spirit.

> For as many as are led by the Spirit of God, they are the sons of God. For ye have not received the spirit of bondage again to fear; but ye have received the Spirit of adoption, whereby we cry, Abba, Father.

The Spirit itself beareth witness with our spirit, that we are the children of God (Rom. 8:14-16).

You, as a child of God, are to be led by the Spirit of God. It is natural for you. It should not be bizarre or unusual for you to be led by the Spirit of God.

So many times people hear a minister or a Christian leader talk about God's leading, and they say, "Well, they are special." I want to tell you that God doesn't choose just pastors to lead. The Bible says, "As many as are led by the Spirit of God, they are the sons of God" (Rom. 8:14).

The reverse of that is also true. As many as are the sons [and daughters] of God, they are led of the Spirit of God. Say it aloud, "I am led of God's Spirit."

You are God's special child. You did not receive the spirit of bondage (see v. 14). You literally have been adopted into His family (see v. 15) and can cry out, "Abba, Father." That's like saying "Daddy" or "Papa." It represents the close relationship between a father and his child.

The Scripture is filled with God's promises of guidance.

My sheep hear my voice, and I know them, and they follow me (John 10:27).

A stranger will they not follow, but will flee from him: for they know not the voice of strangers (John 10:5).

The steps of a good man are ordered by

the Lord (Ps. 37:23).

I [the Lord] will guide thee with mine eye (Ps. 32:8).

Trust in the Lord with all thine heart; and lean not unto thine own understanding. In all thy ways acknowledge him, and he shall direct thy paths (Prov. 3:5-6).

Avoidable Mistakes

A few days ago I was thinking about a family I know who had experienced great personal tragedy in their lives. I asked the Lord, "Why did that happen?" Inside of my spirit came the answer.

The Lord said, "They did not listen to their spirit." The tragedy was avoidable. It didn't have to happen.

I mentioned it to my wife, Sharon, and she said, "Well, of course!" She had known the individuals when they committed their lives to the Lord, but they had since grown cold, indifferent and calloused. They stopped responding to the Spirit of God, and so they walked right into a disastrous situation.

As I pondered that, the Lord said to me, "You must teach the people how to listen to their spirit."

First Corinthians 6:17 says, "He that is joined unto the Lord is one spirit." When you are born again, the Holy Spirit comes to dwell in your spirit. You receive the Spirit of God. We can only cry "Jesus is Lord!" by the Holy Spirit. It is His Spirit in us that causes our spirit to be alive.

Remember what Romans 8:16 says: "The Spirit itself beareth witness with our spirit, that we are the children of God."

In other words, God communicates with us Spirit to spirit. "Bearing witness with our spirit" means He speaks to us in our spirits. That is why we must learn to listen to our spirit.

The Spirit of God tells your spirit that you are God's child — affirms you, confirms you, assures you. He is also the One who will confirm to you God's direction for your life. He will lead you when you learn to listen to Him speaking inside of you.

I can think of three situations in which people I knew personally were attending church, doing well in the Lord and being blessed. Each had opportunities to move to other cities. In their hearts they did not want to leave, but because of an increase in salary, promotion or economic opportunity, the move was made.

In each situation there was disaster: a broken home, rebellion in family members and health problems. All three returned saying, "We made a mistake."

What happened? Did God miss it? Did God fail? Did God drop them? Did God forget them? Or was God speaking to them when their hearts cried out, "I really don't want to go"?

You see, God *is* speaking. Twenty-four hours a day He is broadcasting to our spirits. We need to get our *radio* — our spirit-radio — turned on and tuned in.

Who Knows Best?

I remember when Sharon and I first got started in

11

the ministry in January 1976. The Holy Spirit told me we were to travel to churches of different denominations and that God would open the doors. We had a tremendous financial blessing that allowed us to purchase a van. In addition, the van was available to us at a great price, reduced from what the person had invested in it.

We felt good about it, but we had counsel from others who said, "You don't want to stay in anyone's home when you're traveling on the road. You want your own private place where you can be together and not have to be subject to whatever is going on in people's homes. You need to buy a trailer." They told us about this great trailer deal and took us to see it. They admonished us that this was a great opportunity, and we needed to buy it.

Being willing to comply with what other people seemed to know was best, we bought the trailer. Do you know what happened? It sat unused in a church parking lot. We never slept in it. Do you know why? Our car couldn't pull it!

After we had been on the road a while, we realized some other things as well. Because I hadn't preached much, I didn't have a lot of sermons. I had to read and study every day if I was going to have a different message from the one I had preached the night before.

I spent hours praying, studying and reading. As a result, I wasn't much company to Sharon. Sharon needed somebody to talk to. She didn't resent being in someone else's home. In fact, she loved it. She enjoyed being able to talk and share with pastors' wives. It was a great comfort not to be alone. At the end of that time there was no doubt in our minds that we needed a van, not a trailer.

I still laugh when I think about that trailer sitting unused as a testimony of missing God. It taught me to listen to my spirit.

I want to say this to you about "missing it" when you don't listen to your spirit. The good news is that God is a God of redemption. Aren't you glad to hear that?

The end of my story is that God redeemed us. Five months later we sold the trailer for all that we had put in it. We also got a great deal on a van — not the original one but another. We could pack all of our luggage and books in it, and then we just changed homes every week — sometimes twice a week — as we traveled and ministered.

Our spirits had told us ahead of time what was the right decision to make. We knew it, but we didn't listen to our spirits. How many times have you learned that your hindsight is a lot better than your foresight? But the Spirit of God can give you hindsight in advance. God has already been there; He knows. Though our minds may not be able to comprehend, our spirits have the insight we need for the decisions we are making.

Jesus said, "When he, the Spirit of truth, is come, he will guide you into all truth: for he shall not speak of himself; but whatsoever he shall hear, that shall he speak: and he will shew you things to come" (John 16:13-14).

The Holy Spirit will reveal things in your future you need to know. That doesn't mean everything in your future is going to be revealed to you. There are certainly some things that will happen without God giving you prior notice, but His grace will be sufficient to handle them. He will show us those things that we do need to know. The Spirit of God desires to direct our lives to the place we are to be at just the time we are to be there.

His Will Is Good

There are a few things you need to understand about listening to your spirit. First of all, God's will for you is good. He wants to

- save you (2 Pet. 3:9)

- heal you (1 Pet. 2:24, Matt. 8:16-17)

- empower you with the Holy Spirit (Acts 1:8)

- bless you with Abraham's blessings (Gal. 3:14)

- protect you (Ps. 23)

- preserve you (Ps. 121)

- deliver you (Ps. 37:40; 91)

It is God's will that you would be pure, holy and righteous; that your life would be free; and that you would have victory on the inside.

Now that you know God's will for you, then realize this: God has already made provisions for everything we need. First He guides, then He provides. In 2 Peter 1:3a we read, "His divine power hath given unto us all things that pertain unto life and godliness."

How does He give us these things? "Through the

knowledge of him that hath called us to glory and virtue" (v. 3b). In other words, by knowing Jesus Christ as our Lord and Savior.

Philippians 4:19 says that God will supply all our needs according to His riches in glory *by Christ Jesus.*

Always remember: when God guides, He provides. He won't tell you to do something and then ask you to do it in your own strength. He supplies everything you need through Jesus Christ.

The most exciting part of my Christian walk has been learning to experience God's guidance and provision. I want to share with you in the next few chapters some of the opportunities God has given me to follow His leading.

Some decisions in my life seemed insignificant by themselves. But as I look back, I realized God was setting me up for His plans for my life.

God does phenomenal things when we learn to recognize His guidance and obey Him. God made that truth clear to me during one of the most moving experiences of my life on a cold, snowy January night in Russia in 1992.

CHAPTER TWO

SEEING NEW THINGS

L ord, these people are so precious to You. Give me Your words to say to them tonight." I often prayed that way before my sermons, but this time was a little different. I was seated in the sports arena in St. Petersburg, Russia, gazing in wonder at 18,000 Russians who had come that night seeking God's answers for their lives.

My mind was focused on preaching the message and praying for the people. It took me totally by surprise when the Spirit spoke: "If you had not gone to ORU, you would not be here tonight."

Had I not obeyed the Spirit's leading to attend the college He had chosen for me, this crusade in Russia would never have happened. The training, preparation and open doors would not have been in place.

That decision in my youth to leave southern Arkansas was a pivotal point in my life. The issue was God's calling. He wanted me to separate myself for His service. He had been guiding me to this point all my life.

Personal Salvation

When I was growing up in Magnolia, Arkansas, my parents took me to church where I learned many Bible stories. My heart was tender toward God, but I lacked a personal experience with Jesus.

Several events led to a genuine salvation experience when I was a teenager. In the spring of 1970, a high school senior gave his testimony one Sunday morning at our church and talked about his personal relationship with Jesus. As president of my church's youth group, I was quite uncomfortable listening to someone who really knew Jesus. I was convicted by the Holy Spirit but was too proud to respond to the altar call.

That incident began a time of soul-searching for me. There was a genuine sorrow in my heart for sin as I realized my emptiness. It was a time of brokenness as God made me realize His mercy.

One day at school I received a booklet entitled *The Four Spiritual Laws*. I read:

1. God loves you.

   For God so loved the world, that he gave his only begotten Son, that whosoever believeth in him should not perish, but have everlasting life (John 3:16).

2. Sin has separated you from God.

   For all have sinned, and come short of the glory of God (Rom. 3:23).

3. Jesus died for your sins.

   But God commendeth his love toward us, in that, while we were yet sinners, Christ died for us (Rom. 5:8).

4. You must receive Jesus as your Savior.

   But as many as received Him, to them He gave the right to become children of God (John 1:12, NKVJ).

In my speech class later that spring, our final assignment was a seven-minute extemporaneous speech with four points. I decided to speak on the four steps to salvation from the booklet. I had to memorize all of the information because the speech had to be given without notes. God had set me up!

Until now, I didn't clearly understand all that needed to happen to be born again. God in His grace was leading me to that place where I would fully surrender to Him.

It happened shortly after my speech, on a sunny day in May, 1970. I was driving my '48 black Pon-

day in May 1970. I was driving my '48 black Pontiac Silver Streak car down to the Lion service station to get some gas. As I pulled up to the tanks, I saw one of the people whom I respected most in the world: Jim Davis. He was parked on the opposite side of the "regular" tank.

He smiled when he saw me and said, "Hi, Billy Joe." Then he became a little more serious. "I'm just getting ready to leave." He had just graduated from college, and I could see his car was loaded with all his personal belongings.

Jim had reached out to me as a friend during the four years he attended Southern State College in Magnolia, Arkansas, where I grew up. His freshman year at college was my ninth-grade year in school, and we had both participated in a Christian youth musical. I had dropped out of the musical, but not before meeting Jim. While he was in college, I would see him and he was always friendly.

Realizing it was also my graduation week, Jim reached into his car and pulled out an old brown radio and gave it to me. I had received many new gifts for graduation, but that old radio got to me. Standing between the ethyl and the regular, tears came to my eyes as I held the radio. Today, I know it was the Holy Spirit using Jim's act of love to pull down the final barriers to a genuine salvation experience in my life.

I invited Jim to my house for lunch. After eating and saying good-bye to my folks, Jim asked me a couple of powerful questions. "Are you really saved?" "Have you been born again?"

By now I knew where I stood with God, and I said, "No."

He asked, "Do you want to be saved?"

I replied, "Yes."

He led me in a simple prayer, during which I repented of my sins, confessed Jesus as Lord and invited Him to live in my heart. The moment it happened, I knew I was forgiven. The glory of God filled me. Peace, joy and love as I had never known came inside as the Holy Spirit imparted the life of God into my heart.

From that day on my life went in a new direction. I was truly a new creation. There were lots of struggles, but I knew Jesus was in my heart.

Seeing New Things

After I was saved, I began to see things differently — especially the new preacher's daughter at Jackson Street United Methodist Church. I was a high school graduate and she was a senior. Sharon Swift was one of the funniest girls I had ever met. She was the life of the party wherever she went and loved to talk and tell jokes. We were friends in the youth group, but I never thought about dating her.

Everything changed the day I was saved. My eyes were opened to see the grace of God on Sharon. She had real joy in her life. She loved all kinds of people with a genuine and sincere love. She had character that was a product of her relationship with Jesus.

Immediately I wanted to talk to her at our youth and church services. I even gave her a ride in my Pontiac Silver Streak. Just two or three weeks after my salvation, our youth group went to Six Flags amusement park in Dallas. Sharon and I held hands, rode the rides and stayed together the whole day. Already I was in love with her.

The very night our group arrived home from Six Flags, my family and I left on a trip for Florida to visit my brother, who was in the Air Force. About an hour down the road, somewhere in the woods of north Louisiana, I was staring out the window when a picture formed in front of my eyes. It was a vision of Sharon and me standing together married, preaching to masses of people.

Remember, I had just gotten saved and didn't have a lot of perspective on what visions were or if they could even occur. I did a lot of praying on the rest of that trip.

I didn't tell anyone what had happened, but I made sure I saw plenty of Sharon. As soon as I arrived back from Florida, I called her and asked her out on a date. She replied, "Let me check my calendar." While I waited, she covered the phone and laughed. Then she said, "I think I can work you in between 7:30 and 10:00."

That summer I was at the Swift home almost every night except when we had church or I had a baseball game. It was a time of romance and love in Jesus that I had never experienced before.

Sharon and I continued to date as I attended Southern State College, just a mile away from my house, on a football scholarship.

The next year — the fall of 1971 — was a disturb-ing time for me in the midst of apparent success. I started on the football team as a sophomore, and we won nine of eleven games. My grades were A's and B's. I had a full scholarship, home cooking when I wanted it, my own car and a beautiful girlfriend. Yet inside I was in turmoil.

I did not understand why I was so discontented. I went to the youth/music director at the local Southern Baptist Church just to talk. I couldn't even put into words what I felt, but his encouragement was important.

I also went to the college guidance counselor to seek direction. I even took an aptitude test trying to determine the career direction I should pursue.

But the most important searching of my heart took place in the evenings as I would walk alone on the college athletic fields in prayer. I was desperate to have peace in my heart. I later realized I was unhappy because what I was doing did not satisfy me on the inside.

Eternal Value

One afternoon that fall I was standing in full gear on the football practice field behind the stadium. The offense was running plays and I was on defense playing safety. It happened in just a second.

Before my eyes I saw millions of people living for things that had no eternal value. They would pursue an education in order to get a job so they could buy a house and car and get married. They would have children and raise them to get an education and pursue things. Then I saw them living to retire and buy a house on a lake and a boat. After that they died. As the people died, the Lord spoke and said, "Nothing they have done will go into eternity."

I was nineteen years old and the Lord showed me a choice I could make at this point. I could choose to do what Jesus wanted me to do and be guided by

Him from place to place through life and touch people with His love. It wasn't that I wouldn't have things, but they would not be my reason for living. God gives us the freedom to choose His way or our own. We can choose the blessing or the curse (Deut. 30:19).

As I would come to the end of my life, I would not be counting all the things I had accumulated. Instead, I would look back and see the people who had been touched and I would hear the Lord say, "They will all go into eternity." In other words, they would not be lost but saved.

All of this happened in a flash. I had seen a vision of America as God sees it. I saw people who lived only for material, perishable things. I saw the results of an empty life.

The day I saw that vision on the football field, I made my decision to live for God. I would follow His leading every step of my life and seek to touch people with His love

CHAPTER THREE

EXPERIENCING GOD'S PROVISION

During that sophomore year in 1971, everything in my life seemed perfect from the outside, but I had no peace. Colossians 3:15 says, "Let the peace of God rule in your hearts." God will guide us with His peace or the lack of it in our hearts. One night as I was asking the Lord what was wrong with me, it became clear in my heart that I was to leave Southern State and transfer to another college.

Just before Thanksgiving, I took Sharon to a local

restaurant. It was the only time we had ever eaten at this place and it turned out to be a divine en counter. I soon learned divine encounters are an other way God leads us. While eating a hamburger, I looked up to see an old friend, Ken Barker, walk ing in the door. "I've been wanting to see you," he told me.

My response came as a surprise to me: "I've been wanting to see you, too." It was the Holy Spirit who had prepared me for this God-arranged meeting that would change the course of my life.

I went to Ken's house later that week, and he told me about the college he was attending: Oral Roberts University, in Tulsa, Oklahoma. The goal of the university, Ken said, was to raise up students to hear God's voice — to go where His light is seen dim, His voice is heard small and His power is not known.

That was what I wanted! I was fed up with the emptiness I saw around me. Living for "things" was a dead-end street. I wanted my life to count for eternity.

The vision on the football field, the discontent within me and the divine encounter with Ken all pointed in the same direction. I was to leave my hometown, my family, my girlfriend, a full athletic scholarship and my place on the team. I was to go to a city I had never visited and a school I had just heard about from one person.

I had no idea who Oral Roberts was other than an evangelist like Billy Graham. I had enough money for only one semester at ORU, and yet I was giving up a free ride at Southern State. At the time the schools had approximately the same enrollment.

But God is *Jehovah Jireh,* the God who provides. He sees our need and makes provision for it. As we obey His voice, we discover His provision on the path of obedience. It is very simple   where God guides, He provides.

In the early days of my ministry, God gave me a poem about this revelation:

When God guides, He provides.
What God directs, He protects.
Blessings untold, are waiting for you
As God guides and directs things you do.

Trust in the Lord with your heart, I say.
You'll hear His voice, This is the Way.
Desires from Him, they will come
Your heart bears witness, this is the One.

Vision accomplished, desire achieved.
Results of a heart, willing to believe.
God's plans unfolding as a dream in the
    night
Your acceptance guarantees His power
    and might.

The struggle is over, the battle is done
When you've waited in prayer, to hear
    from the Son.
His voice is clear, the Captain has spoken.
Go forward now! The enemy's power is
    broken.

Rest for you is a way of life.
Gone are the days of worry and strife.

You've come to the place of knowing His
way.
God's plans are blessed, for you to believe and say.

"How Are You Making It Financially?"

While talking with Ken, I thought about the cost
of attending a private university. Ken's father, like
mine, was an accountant and I knew his family was
not in a position to pay for his schooling. My brothers and I had understood we would have to pay for
our own college education. Our parents were very
supportive, but extra money was not available for
tuition, much less room and board in another state
for a private university.

I asked Ken, "How are you making it financially?"
His words planted faith in me that is still producing
miracles today. He said, "Billy Joe, God is my Father
and He cares about me. He owns the cattle on a
thousand hills [Ps. 50:10]. When I am doing what
He has told me to do, He meets all my needs according to His riches in glory by Christ Jesus [Phil.
4:19]."

His words exploded in my heart. I knew God was
my Father, but I had never realized He was concerned for me in such a practical way that He
would provide financially for a need in my life.
However, it clicked in me when Ken spoke about
doing God's will. It made sense. If a soldier goes to
war on behalf of his country, the country takes
responsibility for providing the funds to make sure
the soldier is trained and supplied.

Opposition

My excitement over following God's plan for my life was strong, but I was not prepared for the reaction I would get from others.

First I told Sharon, who said I shouldn't go at the start of the second semester because she wouldn't be able to go with me. Her music classes were such that if she left at midyear, she would lose all her credits from the first semester.

My parents were kind but practical. They said I could not afford to give up my full scholarship and I could never pay the price of tuition, room and board at ORU. They also didn't want their youngest child to leave Magnolia like my two older brothers had done.

My football coach was the hardest one to tell. He had given me such a wonderful opportunity to play on a team that had the potential of winning championships in the next two years. He asked me why I wanted to go to Tulsa. I told him of the spiritual emphasis at ORU, and his response was, "Do they have a corner on religion there? Couldn't you get it here?"

In the natural realm, his comments made sense. I fumbled in my response to him because I did not fully understand the call of God. Finally I said, "All I know is that I'm supposed to go there." It was yet another pull on my sense of loyalty, this time to my team and friends.

It took almost a month from the night I had met with Ken until I finally decided I would go, in spite of all the opposition. But it was a major turning point in my life. For me, it was the moment I had decided to leave everything that had been dear to me to follow Jesus. Normally, going away to college is routine for most people, but my circumstances forced a decision requiring me to deliberately leave father, mother, hometown, girlfriend, college, friends and money. I had just enough in savings for one semester, and in January 1972 I left Arkansas for Tulsa and Oral Roberts University.

No More Loneliness

During that first semester at ORU, many of my nights were spent walking the campus, talking to God. It seemed He had planned this special time with me. Because of transferring at midterm, I didn't know many students, and I was involved in just a few activities. Also, with my girlfriend 325 miles away, I had lots of time to pray.

God was setting me apart for His service. God calls people to do His work. We can either disobey as Jonah did and end up in the belly of a fish on a deep-sea cruise, or we can obey as Daniel did and end up in the lion's den. In either case, if we turn to the Lord in full obedience and trust in His Word, we will be delivered.

It was such a total change for me that there was no loneliness. My life prior to this had been absorbed in sports, dating and studies. Now my focus was changing to living for God.

There were lots of struggles with temptations and feelings of inadequacy. It seemed I was daily in the operating room of the Holy Spirit because there was so much in me that needed changing.

A Lesson on Faith

During that semester, just as I had expected, I used up all my money. Every penny I had saved since I was eleven years old was completely gone. I had two more years to go and no finances in hand to cover the costs.

I took a part-time job in the men's gym class laundry room. One of the other workers, Don Shields, became a close friend. He was in his late twenties, married, with several years of experience in business. He also had transferred to ORU in January.

Realizing I needed more than a part-time job, I began to explore other possibilities on campus. I felt strongly about a position for the following year as a resident advisor supervising thirty-two guys on a dorm floor. This job was ministry-oriented and would pay for half of all my costs during the next school year. I applied for one of the ten to fifteen openings along with more than sixty other ORU male students.

In my heart I felt sure I would get one of the positions as a resident advisor. The day the list was posted in the snack bar area, I ran to see my name. To my disappointment I had not been chosen.

Having been on campus for only two months, I was basically unknown. Most of those applying had been at ORU for over a year and a half. But it was a letdown, and it caused me to wonder about my ability to hear God.

Mammon or the Master?

A summer job opened for me in my hometown

30

working with an oil company for a salary that was almost three times more than minimum wage. I thought it would be a big help toward school in the fall.

About two weeks later, though, I heard that there was a youth pastor position available in DeQueen, Arkansas. The pastor, David Wilson, offered me the position at minimum wage and I had to pay for my own room and board. But, the peace of God came and I sensed Him calling me to accept the position.

However, if I took the job, I would not have enough money for even one more semester at ORU. The Lord tested me to believe Him. Would I obey God and trust Him to provide even though I could not see how it could happen? If God were guiding me, would He also provide for me?

During the past semester Oral Roberts had taught on seed faith. Every seed reproduces after its kind. If you had a need in your life, you could plant a seed in faith with something you did have, and God would multiply it back to you. This is what God did in giving His Son to reap a harvest of many sons and daughters. Through seed faith, there is no need too great that God cannot meet. As we release what is in our hands to God, He releases what is in His hands to us.

In a flash God opened my heart and mind to understand that if I would give myself to serve Him that summer, He would provide all of my educational expenses. My giving up the oil field job was a seed of something I had that represented money. It wasn't necessary for me to know how God would provide. All I needed to do was be faithful to plant the seed by obeying God

After telling Pastor Wilson I would take the position in DeQueen, I learned that a group in the church had taken a special offering to cover the costs of my summer room and board. Praise God! The miracles had begun.

Summer of Miracles

That summer was a time of wonderful ministry with the teenagers at First United Methodist Church. But at the same time I had to "cast down" thoughts of not having finances for school in the fall (2 Cor. 10:5).

God doesn't always settle up every Friday. He calls us to walk by faith and trust His Word regardless of what we see. After we have obeyed the word of the Lord, the key issue is to remain steadfast. "Cast not away therefore your confidence, which hath great recompence of reward. For ye have need of patience, that, after ye have done the will of God, ye might receive the promise" (Heb. 10:35-36).

The summer of 1972 was a proving ground for my faith in Jesus. Would I stay true to obeying Him at all costs? For me, there was no other way to go. Only a miracle could make it possible to continue at ORU.

In mid-July I received an unusual letter from my laundry room friend, Don Shields. His wife had gotten a job at ORU as secretary to the dean of men. As summer started, the assistant dean left his job and the dean needed a replacement. He asked his secretary, Don's wife, if she knew any good candidates, and she suggested her husband. The dean hired him, and one of his first assignments was to oversee the resident counselor program.

Only days into the job, Don was notified that one of the student resident counselors was leaving to join the Navy. As Don was faced with filling the position, he reviewed the list of almost fifty remaining candidates who had applied in the spring. Since he had only been at ORU one semester, I was the only one he knew!

Praise God! Don wrote offering me the job as resident adviser, which covered half of my costs at ORU for an entire year. I felt like Joseph being called up from prison to serve in Pharaoh's court — out of the laundry room and into a staff position at ORU!

A couple of weeks later I received a letter from ORU's financial aid department. I had been awarded an academic scholarship that would cover the other half of my expenses. Glory to God! The money I earned that summer became spending money for the school year.

Through personal experience I learned the meaning of the verse "Whatever a man sows, that he will also reap...In due season we shall reap if we do not lose heart" (Gal. 6:7,9, NKJV). It gave me the faith I needed to meet the new challenges in my life.

CHAPTER FOUR

EXPERIENCING FAITH

Sharon joined me at ORU in the fall of 1972, and in the spring of 1973 I asked her to marry me. We set the wedding date in August. That spring we were both in school and heavily involved in many activities. Our time was so stretched that we neglected our daily devotions of prayer and Bible study.

About a month after our engagement, the Holy Spirit warned me that if we were married in our present spiritual condition, our marriage would not last.

There are so many opportunities in life to become busy doing things for the Lord that we neglect our relationship with Him. When we're in that condition, we risk losing God's blessing even though we're doing things He has told us to do.

As I sought the Lord, it became clear to me that Sharon and I needed to end the engagement and seek Jesus. We broke it off amidst lots of tears, but in the end we got things right with the Lord in our daily schedules and private devotions. God then released us to resume our marriage plans.

Faith for an Apartment

The spring before our wedding we sat down to estimate our costs to live in Tulsa and attend ORU. We decided to believe God for an apartment renting for $65 a month, bills paid. This was extremely low, even in 1973.

One evening I took Sharon to a restaurant in the area where we were looking for an apartment. We had driven around, but didn't know exactly what we were searching for. We noticed an older lady sitting all alone in the restaurant and our hearts were moved to join her. She was delighted to have someone to talk with as she ordered two meals and ate both.

She told us about some problems she had with an apartment she rented out, and our ears perked right up. She said it was a garage apartment she rented for $65 a month. Everything in me tingled with excitement as she spoke — I realized God had miraculously led us to the apartment for which we had prayed. Hearing of our plans to be married in

August, she was unsure if it would be available in time. Amazingly, her renter moved out at the end of July and in plenty of time for our arrival. What a mighty God we serve!

The Angel of the Lord

The week we moved into the little garage apartment, the neighbors came over to greet us. The man related how there had been several robberies in the area. Just two doors down, someone had pulled a truck up to the house and stolen the furniture!

Even though the only furniture we owned was two director's chairs and a lamp, I didn't want anyone taking them. The thought of robbers coming to our little place began to fill my mind with worry and fear.

One night I lay in bed thinking of a plan of escape if the bad guys came to our door. I could envision the thieves approaching our home. The wind was blowing leaves down the street and rattling the iron gate outside. It sounded just like a prowler was opening the gate and coming into our yard.

Oppressive thoughts of fear kept me awake past midnight until a scripture rose up from my spirit and into my mind: "The angel of the Lord encampeth round about them that fear him, and delivereth them" (Ps. 34:7).

I jumped up in our bed and shouted, "Hallelujah!"

Then it was Sharon I had to calm down as she woke up wondering what I was yelling about. Since that day, faith has replaced fear.

Faith believes God's Word while fear believes the oppressive lies of Satan and circumstances. Faith can drive out fear by speaking and acting on the truth. Fear paralyzes while faith liberates. To have faith in God is the only way to real and complete freedom.

I had allowed a sequence of words and natural circumstances to paint a picture in my mind of something terrible. Fear creates images just as faith does. The image you hold in your mind will eventually dominate your spirit to obey God or turn from Him. No wonder Jesus said "Fear not" over and over again.

Transportation Provided

During that school year I worked for a local church. Sharon and I had a miracle provision in the city bus system changing its routes the summer before we moved into the apartment. We lived six miles from ORU, and only one bus route went by the campus at that time. Amazingly, that route was switched in the summer of 1973 to go directly by our apartment to and from ORU. I was able to catch the bus and go to work while Sharon kept the car for her late music rehearsals.

In December the pastor I worked for informed me that I needed to start hospital visitation after Christmas. With our class schedules and obligations, it seemed impossible, but I accepted my assignment, and we prayed for a miracle.

A few days later my brother Charles called and said he was being transferred to Clark Air Force

Base in the Philippines. He asked if I could keep his car for a year. Of course, you know what we said! On New Year's weekend he brought me his Pontiac Bonneville and a credit card to pay for all the oil and gas for a year. Hallelujah! Where God guides, He provides!

Experiencing the Word

During my last semester at ORU I realized my need to know the Bible even more. God put in my heart a desire for His Word to be in my life.

I was working at a local church which had offered me a full-time position upon graduation. I had also applied and been accepted to work with Youth for Christ as a regional director.

Just weeks before graduation I was sitting in a Christian education class when I heard my professor, Dr. Durasoff, mention a youth director position opening at a church in town. Immediately the Spirit bore witness that it was my job. When class dismissed, I ran to the nearest phone and called the church, Sheridan Christian Center.

A time was arranged for Sharon and me to come "try out" for the position. We were to speak at a midweek service to their youth group in the presence of the pastor. Only fifteen teens showed up, and the pastor was unable to make it. The situation looked even bleaker after I called the pastor, who said no decision was being made at the time.

As I prayed during the last part of April 1974, it came to me to release the two sure job offerings because we were called to be the youth leaders at Sheridan. The Holy Spirit guides us when we cannot see any reason to do what we are doing.

It was very strange graduating from college and giving up two good ministry positions to wait on God's best. The last night we were to be in Tulsa, I called the pastor of Sheridan, Glenn Millard, to let him know where we would be if they decided to select us as youth pastors. He said they had not found anyone yet.

After a pause he said, "Why don't you come and work with us and see if you like us and we like you." With that word, God's direction was confirmed for our lives

When the Lord provided me with a job as youth pastor at Sheridan Christian Center in Tulsa, little did we know how that calling would develop in the coming years.

First of all, we heard about a camp meeting with Kenneth Hagin, a Bible teacher who travelled in ministry. The meetings were held the last week of July and we went. The Word of God was spoken with authority as people taught of believing, speaking and acting on God's promises. The message was simple, yet profound: God's Word is true and you can live by it.

The things we had learned at ORU were reinforced as we began to understand more of God's Word. Joy, peace, victory, healing and blessing began to flow in our lives as we started believing the Word of God.

My biggest struggle was accepting that it was God's will for all to be healed. For six months I challenged this idea by diligently searching the four Gospels. I knew that Jesus had come to do the Father's will and speak the Father's words. Jesus revealed God's will in what He said and did. There was no place in the Gospels that He made anyone sick or told anyone to stay sick for God's glory. Everywhere He went people were healed, delivered and set free as they came to Him in faith.

Some people told me that God told the apostle Paul he was to be sick. I studied the passage to see for myself if that is what the Bible said. I read:

> And lest I should be exalted above measure by the abundance of the revelations, a thorn in the flesh was given to me, a messenger of Satan to buffet me, lest I be exalted above measure.
>
> Concerning this thing I pleaded with the Lord three times that it might depart from me. And He said to me, "My grace is sufficient for you, for My strength is made perfect in weakness." Therefore most gladly I will rather boast in my infirmities, that the power of Christ may rest upon me (2 Cor. 12:7-9, NKJV).

Notice the phrase "messenger of Satan" (v. 7). It was not from God but from the devil. It was not a sickness but a demonic spirit sent to oppose Paul in the ministry. The word *messenger* in the Greek is *angelos*. It is translated as either "angel" or "messenger" in the Bible, but it always refers to a being and not a condition.

Paul asked the Lord to remove this demonic opposition three times. Notice the Lord's response: "My grace is sufficient for you, for My strength is made perfect in weakness" (v. 9). God assured Paul that he had already been given God's help and ability (grace) to handle any opposition the devil threw at him. Instead of removing the devil, God made Paul stronger in grace to overcome. No wonder Paul said he took pleasure in those difficult moments, because God's strength increased with each difficult situation.

As I studied the verses in the Bible about healing, I saw that God's will was health and wholeness. Yet it became clear that not all people would be healed and not all would be saved But that did not change God's will for salvation or healing

When I settled it in my heart concerning God's will to heal, my other doubts about God's Word vanished. The issue of healing has a domino effect on other areas of your faith. It makes sense once you see the big picture. If the enemy can get you to doubt God's Word on healing, he can tempt you to doubt in other areas such as divine protection, di vine provision and salvation of family members

A Vision of the Future

Brother Hagin started Rhema Bible Training Center in the fall of 1974 at Sheridan Christian Center. Since Ken Jr.'s office was across the hall from mine, we had an opportunity to become friends, and he opened the classroom to me. I was able to sit in on classes for a year and a half.

For the first year there was a monthly seminar at Sheridan with a special guest teacher. As one of those guests, Kenneth Copeland, was speaking, I had another vision. I saw myself standing behind the pulpit in the very place Brother Copeland was standing. I then heard the Lord say, "You will be the next pastor of this church."

The moment this happened, Brother Copeland began to prophesy, "The days will come when this church will burst out of its walls and touch the whole world."

Though I was stunned by what I had seen and heard, my heart agreed with it. Sharon was the only one I told about the vision until it was fulfilled four years later It's not totally clear to me why God showed me this in advance The vision certainly was not a merit badge or a sign of achievement, but it did help guide my decisions and actions. (I will share a lot more about visions and their purpose in chapter 16.)

A Word in the Night

One night in March 1975, I was lying in bed at midnight praying in the Spirit.

Paul said, "For if I pray in an unknown tongue, my spirit prayeth, but my understanding is unfruitful. What is it then? I will pray with the spirit, and I will pray with the understanding also..." (1 Cor. 14:14-15).

I sensed something special was stirring in my spirit, and I began to seek God's interpretation as I prayed in English. The words began to flow out: "I have called you to travel — teaching and preaching. I will open the doors of denominational churches to you."

There was more the Lord spoke to me, but this was the heart of the direction. We had moved from a denominational background to a nondenominational setting. There were things we had learned that God wanted us to share with people who had never heard them.

I had no idea at the time of the massive worldwide revival in denominational churches. We were to be a tiny piece of the outpouring that would bridge continents, races and centuries of tradition.

As I reflected on the word of the Lord, it seemed practical that I should enroll formally in the Rhema Bible Training Center in September to complete its training program the following May. This would enable me to launch out preaching in June 1976. For the next two months, in the spring of 1975, I had a strong desire to teach and preach more than the youth services. Since our first vacation was coming up in June, we decided to accept offers to preach that had come our way and scheduled our entire vacation to be on the road ministering.

As I prayed one afternoon, I could not get my mind off traveling and preaching the Word. It was so strong that I could not concentrate on a message I was to give that night. Finally I said, "God, why are You bugging me?"

Immediately the Spirit in me spoke strongly, "January!"

I said, "January? OK." I suddenly realized God did not want me waiting another year to get going. It was as clear as a bell, and I accepted it. My practical plan to finish Rhema and go on the road in June was not God's plan.

There is nothing wrong with making plans and being practical. But when God shows you another direction, obey it

CHAPTER FIVE

HANDLING OPPOSITION

God also gave me a word that helped me for the six months prior to beginning our traveling ministry. He said, "You will have more places to go than you have time to go." I began to say that to myself every time thoughts of fear or worry tried to enter my mind.

As I thanked the Lord for His promise, a peace filled my heart. When the Lord speaks to you and fear tries to steal away your faith, just let your heart be filled with thanks for what God has given you.

Invite His peace to reign in your life (more on this in chapter 15).

I knew we were going to have exactly what the Lord had spoken, even though it didn't appear that way right up to the time of our departure from Tulsa in December 1975.

Pastor Millard at Sheridan asked me, "Do you have any places to preach?"

It was November and we still didn't have any meetings confirmed.

He said, "Why don't you stay here with us until you have enough places to go full time?"

My reply was, "I believe God has directed us to start full time in January." It was a time to either know we were called or forget it. I knew without a doubt I had heard from God.

A few of the churches where we had spoken during the summer said to call them if we were available again. By the time we left our comfortable, salaried position, we had only two meetings confirmed. The first was a going-away service on New Year's Eve at Sheridan. The second was a two-week meeting at Bethel Church in my hometown of Magnolia, Arkansas.

I also talked to the pastor of my home church who was interested in hearing us speak, but we did not set a date.

Love Always Triumphs

Sheridan Christian Center gave us a warm farewell on New Year's Eve, and the next week we headed for the meetings in Magnolia at Bethel Full Gospel Church. I was in for some surprises.

Many of the people I expected to come never made it to the services at Bethel. On the other hand, lots of folks I had never met came to hear God's Word.

Previously the church had been meeting on the "other side of the tracks" in a forty-year-old white wood-frame building which had burned down only a couple of years before. Now they were dedicating a new brick building on the growing edge of town. More than one thousand first-time visitors came as the meetings stretched into six weeks.

I didn't even have enough sermons for that many meetings! Each day I spent hours studying just to be ready for the evening ministry. It was literally a new message every night for the people and for me.

The forty nights of preaching in our first revival was the confirmation we needed. By the time the meetings ended, other doors opened in several different places.

While we were preaching at Bethel Full Gospel Church, several of the board members from our home church came to hear us. They were surprised to see Sharon and me both praying for the sick to be healed and teaching on the power of the Holy Spirit.

The Saturday morning we were leaving town to speak elsewhere, I decided to call the pastor of our home church and settle the date for us to speak. He said that things had changed and it would probably be better if we did not come.

Stunned, I asked, "Why?"

He said, "Some of our board members attended your services, and they don't feel we are ready for what you are preaching."

My mom was listening in the kitchen and picked up the disappointment in my voice. We all had looked forward to our ministering in the church I had attended from birth. Sharon's father had pastored the church just five years before, my dad had been chairman of the board before his death, and my mom was the adult Sunday school class teacher. She was struck deeply by the rejection of people.

I don't remember ever seeing my mother get that angry before. She said, "I'll never go back to that church. After all we have done for them, and now this."

She felt their rejection of Sharon and me more deeply than we felt it. In fact, I understood the position the pastor and board were taking, even though I knew they were wrong.

As we clung to each other in shock, God took over and Mom agreed to go to church the next day and love the people. She cried through the entire service and especially as she walked in and out of the building greeting her longtime friends (who were board members).

We forgave them and released them from that offense. There was no bitterness or resentment in our hearts. We truly believed God would somehow be glorified. Little did we know just what Jesus had in mind.

About four months later I received a call from the pastor inviting me to conduct a youth weekend retreat, speaking to their teenagers on a Friday and Saturday night. In a half laugh he said, "I'm working on getting you to speak in the Sunday morning service."

We rejoiced and showed up to lead the retreat. The door opened, and I did speak on Sunday morning. It was a simple message, "You Must Be Born Again." Sixty people came to the altar that morning, while two members of the congregation gave a testimony and a prophetic word. The whole place was filled with people weeping and rejoicing. We had learned a great lesson: Love always triumphs.

Sometimes when you're following God's leading you encounter rejection. Jesus was rejected by the religious leaders of His day. His hometown of Nazareth rejected Him after He preached His first message. Because God's ways go against the ways of man, you may encounter some rejection or opposition. If you walk in love and humility, God will bring you through victorious.

"If You Don't Get Bitter"

Just before we started on the road in ministry, I asked Dr. Roy Hicks Sr. the question, "If there was one good thing you could tell me, what would it be?"

Dr. Hicks had been guest speaking at Rhema for the week. He served as superintendent of the International Church of the Foursquare Gospel for a period of time. He also had pastored many years in addition to traveling in the ministry.

As we walked across the parking lot, he said, "If you don't get bitter, you'll make it." He explained that God had given us all we would ever need to succeed, but bitterness could stop His blessings.

Dr. Hicks was a wise man who knew human nature. In our years of ministry, Sharon and I have faced many opportunities to get bitter, but each time we have forgiven. God worked His redemption in every situation.

Joseph was rejected and sold by his own brothers into slavery. He was tempted, slandered and imprisoned even though he was innocent. Human nature doesn't change. It is easy to see that Joseph's biggest challenges were bitterness and unforgiveness. He forgave his brothers and the others because he understood God's great overriding power in his life.

When his brothers begged Joseph to forgive them he said, "Do not be afraid, for am I in the place of God? But as for you, you meant evil against me; but God meant it for good, in order to bring it about as it is this day, to save many people alive" (Gen. 50:19-20, NKJV).

Joseph recognized that God turned the situation for good in spite of the evil intentions of those who had hurt him. Joseph was able to see God instead of the hurt and rejection. He got better instead of bitter. As a result, he went from prisoner to prime minister in one day.

We need to believe no one, no thing and no circumstance can stop us from being right where God wants us to be. His timing is beautiful, and He will fulfill His plan regardless of the opposition.

A Heartbeat of Love

In March 1975 we were ministering at the Pullman Heights United Methodist Church in Hot Springs, Arkansas. As I was reading a Christ for the Nations (CFN) magazine, the Spirit spoke to me that we were to attend CFN's summer session.

Those six weeks in Dallas, Texas, changed us forever. We caught the vision of world missions at the CFN Institute, which was founded in 1970 by

Gordon and Freda Lindsay. As we heard the speakers and saw the pictures of native churches built worldwide, our view of the world exploded.

It became clear to me that I was to be a "world Christian," living for the imperishable rewards of His kingdom. I saw the selfishness of many American Christians and the need to focus on world evangelism.

It was clear that faith, the gifts of the Spirit and the power of God were not to be used for self-centered purposes but rather to meet the needs of others. As love became our heartbeat, we started believing for reaching people of other nations.

It seemed so simple once I clearly saw the Word of God. Jesus left His home in heaven to reach us. He calls His ministers to be willing to leave their homes and reach people. We care about all the world because Jesus died for the whole world. As He was sent, so we are sent. The gift He gave us, we are to give others.

Christ for the Nations helped us at a critical point in our lives to understand the purpose of prosperity. We saw moderation, frugality and humility in action throughout their organization. We learned not to seek blessings for our own personal gain. Those who use the blessings of God to reach the world will be honored, and those with impure motives will be judged.

The principle of seeking God first has been fulfilled in our lives. He gave us everything we needed. We have not lacked because of the Lord's willingness and faithfulness to supply our needs. He has supplied abundantly, and as a result, we have been able to pass blessings on to others.

CHAPTER SIX

WAITING ON A VISION

In January 1977, one year after we started our traveling ministry, I received a call from Phil Derstine, a fellow ORU graduate, asking if we could be the youth directors for the Christian Retreat in northern Minnesota. I explained to him we were traveling as evangelists and weren't doing that type of ministry anymore. I immediately got a knot in my stomach area. It took me a while to realize it was my spirit grieving over a wrong decision.

God leads by His peace. "Let the peace of God

rule in your hearts" (Col. 3:15). The moment our spirit loses the presence of God's peace we should recognize it is the Lord speaking to us. God will warn us if we are headed in a wrong direction. Listen to your spirit.

For the next two weeks I endured a lack of peace until I finally called Phil back and told him we would take the job. Up to this time we had not preached north of Tulsa, but in the two weeks after Phil called, we got an unusual lineup of preaching engagements in Illinois and Wisconsin that lasted from May 1 to June 12. God had already gone ahead of us and arranged our schedule so that we would be in the northern United States just in time to start work at Strawberry Lake.

We had lots of surprises at Christian Retreat. The very first night they asked me to lead singing and Sharon to play the piano for the choruses. Neither of us had done it before. It was a real experience in patience and self-control, not only for us, but also for the audience!

Sharon's primary job was to direct the registration office. She is not the type for office work or accounting, and the job became an ordeal that stretched her to the limit. There was weeping and prayer many a night to get the books to balance.

My job was to teach the morning youth service, drive the ski boat for skiers on occasion, rake leaves, wash dishes, lead worship, sell goodies in the snack shop and lead the volleyball game for teens at night. It was a humbling experience, but I needed it.

Every afternoon I had a one-hour block of free time when I would head for an empty field or white birch forest to get alone and talk with Jesus. One day I asked Him why He brought us to Strawberry Lake and why it was taking so long for the vision to be fulfilled of pastoring in Tulsa. He told me, "I am planting an oak tree. You will stand against the storms."

It became clear to me that God was doing a work in me to remove impurities and allow the true gold to shine in my life. It was painful and joyful all at the same time. The flesh was dying and my selfish desires were being crucified. As Jesus said, "Whosoever will save his life shall lose it: but whosoever will lose his life for my sake, the same shall save it" (Luke 9:24).

I was finding the pure joy of loving Jesus and serving Him regardless of how many people honored me or knew of our work. I realized how dependent I had been on the praise of others. Jesus wanted me to please Him.

The summer of 1977 was perhaps one of the most important training times in my life. I found out a lot about myself in the backwoods of Minnesota, and I saw what God wanted in me.

The Lord told me, "I am more interested in saving you than I am in you saving the world." I had not thought in those terms, but I realized that my efforts to reach others would only be eternally effective if my life was in obedience to Jesus Christ.

The Spirit said to me, "If I put you in that position now [pastoring Sheridan Christian Center], you would be destroyed and you would destroy the church." I realized it's not enough to be in the right place. I must be right inside of my being. The selfish will must be conquered in order to let Jesus have His way.

Jesus assured me I would be in the position He

had revealed, but it would happen when I was ready. I was able to identify with Moses spending forty years on the backside of the desert. The job demanded such strength of character that God took His servant aside from the business of the world to address major flaws in his life. By the time God appeared in the burning bush, Moses' pride was gone and he realized his empty, weak life could not get the job done.

Once we come to the point of knowing we cannot do it, we are ready for God to work. The work *in me* had to be done before God would work *through me* in the way He desired. I don't regret the time and manner in which the Lord worked in my heart at Strawberry Lake. He hasn't stopped the process either; even now He is doing a special work in me. I learned my relationship to Jesus was more important than all the things I might do in ministry.

A retreat speaker preached that motives must be right before miracles will happen — purity precedes power. *I realized that what I am determines what I do.* If I am pure and holy in my heart, then my actions will be pure and holy.

Because of the vision and word of the Lord, I knew a day was coming when Sharon and I would lead many people. But that summer I died to my desire for glory or honor related to a position. All I wanted was Jesus and His will to be done in my life.

"Go Back to Tulsa"

In November 1977 we were speaking for Grady and Rose Barton at their church in Aledo, Texas. As

I prepared for an evening service the Lord spoke to me, "Go back to Tulsa in September, attend Rhema and I will open the door at Sheridan for you to be the pastor."

God makes all things beautiful in His time. The direction was clear. You could say we were taxiing into position for takeoff. Our life had been full of ministry, but in many ways it was simple. The pace and demands were about to accelerate.

Shortly after this word from the Lord, I received a call from Pastor Millard at Sheridan. He asked us to conduct a revival in April. During that series of meetings he said, "If you ever come back to Tulsa, I want you to preach for me on Sundays."

The congregation was unusually receptive to our ministry. When I told Brother Millard we were returning in September to attend Rhema, he seemed excited. We could see the pieces of the puzzle starting to fall into place.

That summer we ministered in Blue Mountain Christian Retreat thirty miles outside of Allentown, Pennsylvania, and also at the Christian Retreat in Bradenton, Florida. Sharon was eight months pregnant with our first child, Sarah, during the twelve-hundred-mile bumpy ride back to Tulsa. A vision from the Lord was about to be fulfilled.

CHAPTER SEVEN

SPIRIT-LED ADMINISTRATION

I began preaching on Sundays for Pastor Millard in Tulsa, and by October he told me he felt I was to be the next pastor. On November 21 they voted us in. We started pastoring in January 1979 with three hundred to four hundred people attending Sunday morning services. The vision I had when Kenneth Copeland was preaching had been fulfilled.

The church went through an explosion of growth to some two thousand in attendance in two years.

To handle the increase, we went to six Sunday services. Victory Christian School and Victory Bible Institute both began that year (1979). We caught a wave of the Spirit that carried us in a flow of salvations, healings and miracles.

In one way I was prepared for the growth because God had spoken in 1974 that it would come. On the other hand, I was overwhelmed with the responsibilities that came with a large, growing congregation and two young schools. The pace was relentless, and I had never managed a staff. Up until now it was just Sharon and me, but suddenly we were in the middle of a glorious move of God filled with demands and pressures coming from all directions.

Sharon and I truly care about people. When we were youth pastors, there were lots of personal contacts and one-on-one ministry with teens. We handled most of the duties related to the youth ministry. I tried to use this same approach in pastoring but ran into lots of problems. I was trying to do it all myself with several times more people and situations to handle.

God sent us hardworking associates in Dave Grothe, Greg Glassford, Mark Turner and Tim O'Leary. Gradually I learned to release responsibilities and delegate authority, but it was a bumpy ride, like going on a roller coaster.

Equip the Believers

Through reading about other ministers, I came across the passage of scripture in Ephesians 4:11-12:

> And he gave some, apostles; and some,
> prophets; and some, evangelists; and
> some, pastors and teachers; for the per-
> fecting of the saints, for the work of the
> ministry, for the edifying of the body of
> Christ.

I realized that my calling was to equip, train and
prepare Christians to do the work of ministry that
God had called them to do. I was not to try and do
it all myself. Even Jesus didn't try to do it all Himself
while He was on earth. He trained twelve and sent
them to do just what He was doing. In addition, He
commissioned seventy others to preach, heal and
deliver.

It came to a climax as I sensed God telling me,
"Let My people go." I was holding them in captivity
by personally assuming all ministry responsibilities.
The Lord let me know that trained believers could
share their faith, win the lost, pray for the sick, give
words of encouragement and show the love of
God.

The week this revelation dawned on me, I stood
in the pulpit on Sunday and told our people, "I'm
ordaining all of you to do the good works of the
Lord." Ephesians 2:10 says:

> For we are his workmanship, created in
> Christ Jesus unto good works, which God
> hath before ordained that we should walk
> in them.

Jesus said we would do even greater works than
He did (John 14:12). Jesus intended that His minis-

try would continue through those who believed in Him. Every believer is to share in the ministry of Jesus. Luke 4 offers a job description of the ministry of Jesus, which has been handed over to us

> The Spirit of the Lord is upon me, because he hath anointed me to preach the gospel to the poor; he hath sent me to heal the brokenhearted, to preach deliverance to the captives, and recovering of sight to the blind, to set at liberty them that are bruised, to preach the acceptable year of the Lord (vv. 18-19).

From that point on, my workload got easier. Others began to pick up part of the load and it was thrilling to see God use people who had done nothing but sit in a pew for years.

Jesus was leading me all the way. Even when I didn't recognize His wisdom and direction, He was guiding my pathway. The struggle I went through now helps me relate to other leaders who are coping with increasing demands.

Going through a struggle does not mean you are out of God's will. The fact that you are facing challenges that require faith and patience often is a sign you are in the center of God's will. The main issue to settle is whether or not you are obeying God. If you are following God's directions, He will provide whatever is needed to see you through to victory.

Delegate

One day I was reading Exodus 18 and Acts 6 and

gained a revelation on organization and delegation. If the Spirit leads you into any kind of leadership position, I guarantee this is a revelation you will need.

After Moses had led over 1.5 million people out of Egypt, he attempted to manage, counsel and govern all of them single-handedly. His father-in-law, Jethro, surveyed the situation and gave him godly advice.

> And so it was, on the next day, that Moses sat to judge the people; and the people stood before Moses from morning until evening. So when Moses' father-in-law saw all that he did for the people, he said, "What is this thing that you are doing for the people? Why do you alone sit, and all the people stand before you from morning until evening?"
>
> And Moses said to his father-in-law, "Because the people come to me to inquire of God. When they have a difficulty, they come to me, and I judge between one and another; and I make known the statutes of God and His laws."
>
> So Moses' father-in-law said to him, "The thing that you do is not good. Both you and these people who are with you will surely wear yourselves out. For this thing is too much for you; you are not able to perform it by yourself (Ex. 18:13-18, NKJV).

I was struck with Jethro's words about wearing out both yourself and the people because the job is too much. I could identify with that.

In my first year of pastoring my schedule went from early morning until late at night, seven days a week. I didn't know how to take a day of rest or get away for a vacation because of all the demands and needs. I felt a constant pressure not to overlook any detail or person that might need attention.

One day as I took a walk, I realized my chest had tightened to the point I had difficulty breathing. The realization hit me that the cares of the ministry, the stress and the demanding schedule had caused the situation. It was time for a change!

Dying young did not appeal to me. It seemed I could help more people if I lived longer.

Jethro, in the wisdom of the Lord, gave Moses a simple plan (Ex. 18:19-23).

1. Pray for all the people. Be an intercessor for them.

2. Teach the people the laws and statutes of God.

3. Teach them the work they must do.

4. Appoint able men to be rulers over thousands, hundreds, fifties and tens who will judge the people and handle their problems.

What Jethro gave Moses was a biblical pattern of delegation. In Acts 6 we also see the early church use Spirit-led delegation when Jerusalem exploded with the new converts and the apostles found themselves with more than they could handle.

And in those days, when the number of the disciples was multiplied, there arose a murmuring of the Grecians against the Hebrews, because their widows were neglected in the daily ministration.

Then the twelve called the multitude of the disciples unto them, and said, It is not reason that we should leave the word of God, and serve tables.

Wherefore, brethren, look ye out among you seven men of honest report, full of the Holy Ghost and wisdom, whom we may appoint over this business.

But we will give ourselves continually to prayer, and to the ministry of the word...

And the word of God increased; and the number of the disciples multiplied in Jerusalem greatly; and a great company of the priests were obedient to the faith (Acts 6:1-4, 7).

The principles are basically the same as in Exodus 18:

1. Give yourself to prayer.

2. Teach the Word of God.

3. Appoint leaders full of the Holy Spirit and wisdom to handle the business.

We realized the revival we were experiencing could keep going if we obeyed the instructions from God's Word. It was clear to me that God did not intend for His ministers to destroy themselves or their families by unrealistic schedules and demands. That's not the way the Spirit leads.

Starting each day in prayer became a priority for my life. Then I began to teach more on the work each member should do in serving the Lord. I encouraged them in their ability to minister to others in witnessing, prayer, counseling, healing and exhortation. It was at this time that we began small group meetings in homes to release more people into ministry.

Timed Right

God was right. If I had been put in leadership at Sheridan Christian Center before spending that time at Strawberry Lake, I would not have been ready for the job. Thank God for His wisdom from the Bible to handle the blessing of growth. It was this period of growth that would put me in the position for the next leading from the Holy Spirit.

CHAPTER EIGHT

LED FORTH
WITH PEACE

As attendance grew at Sheridan, we came to the point where we could not add any more services. Architectural plans were drawn for an enlarged sanctuary on the back of our lot. At the city council hearing for approval of a building permit, we were met by a group of neighbors protesting further expansion that would create more traffic problems. They complained of blocked driveways up and down the bordering streets. We asked for a sixty-day delay on a decision and went to prayer.

It became clear in my spirit that we would not get approval to build. I didn't even go to the final hearing and felt a peace when our administrator returned with the news we were turned down, even though I had no idea what we would do.

As I was praying about the situation that night, I heard the word of the Lord, "Tink Wilkerson's Auto Mart." This was a ten-acre car dealership four miles south of our church on Sheridan Road that had just gone up for sale. I got in my car wearing a coat over my pajamas and drove to the auto mart. That night, January 8, 1981, I stepped out of the car and called that property and buildings into the ministry of the Lord Jesus Christ.

The next day, Friday, I contacted the owners and was given a tour of the facilities. I could see our offices, auditorium and classrooms fitting into the building perfectly. It was suitable for where we were at the time if it could be remodeled.

Our board met me at the property on Saturday to take a look. Excitedly I told them about my word from the Lord and how we could fit our ministry into the auto mart. But I could tell by the expressions on their faces that they did not share my joy. To them it was a car lot with showroom windows and greasy mechanic bays.

As I shared the idea with the church staff and other leaders, they were more supportive. However, in the January board meeting, the men shared kindly about their doubts of this being a move we should make. I was caught in the middle between what I perceived to be the word of the Lord and the opinion of our board.

All of the men respected me and rejoiced in the

church's growth. They voiced repeatedly, "We know we have to do something." Each of us realized that people were being turned away because of the over-crowded auditorium and parking lots. The board had a problem with leaving a building and site that meant so much to them. Most of them had helped start the church.

On the other side there was a growing number of people who had heard of the new idea and were ready to act. These were mostly folks who had joined the church in 1979 and 1980 under our ministry. They sensed the Spirit speaking to us:

> Enlarge the place of your tent, stretch your tent curtains wide, do not hold back; lengthen your cords, strengthen your stakes (Is. 54:2, NIV).

"Go For It!"

Prior to all of this, I had scheduled a trip in the fall to visit Israel in March 1981. With the decision about a relocation up in the air, I had no desire to leave the country and so notified the twelve tour members of our plans to postpone or cancel the trip. One of the men insisted I go through with the Israel trip plans. At the time I didn't realize God was using this man to get me away from the confusion to a place where I could hear Him.

The trip and site visits were enjoyable, with no outstanding events. Each day I would find a place alone to wait on God. While spending a couple of days at the Sea of Galilee, I became relaxed and at peace in my heart. One afternoon, sitting on a beautiful grassy hillside sloping down to the water, I heard the words: "Go for it." They were as clear as a bell and I knew instantly we were to go after the auto mart and begin a new church.

Upon returning, I shared my heart with the board. They asked if I would pastor the new church as well as the old one. They were supportive to the idea of the new church but personally felt they should stay where they were. I did not sense the leading to pastor both places.

One of the men, Howard Dessinger, quoted Matthew 9:17:

> Nor do they put new wine into old wineskins, or else the wineskins break, the wine is spilled, and the wineskins are ruined. But they put new wine into new wineskins, and both are preserved (NKJV).

Howard explained that what was happening was "new wine" that needed a new wineskin. If they would release it, both the old and the new church would be preserved. Thanks to the mercy and leading of the Holy Spirit, we didn't divide — we multiplied.

We set Easter Sunday, April 19, 1981, as our day to begin the new church: Victory Christian Center. Because of the unusual circumstances, we were impressed not to ask anyone at Sheridan to go with us. We only asked the staff if they planned to stay or go with the new church so that we could make plans for staffing.

Sensing the auto mart would not be ready in the three-and-a-half weeks of remodeling, we scheduled

Easter Sunday services in Tulsa's downtown convention center. To our surprise, sixteen hundred people showed up. We wept with tears of joy and gratitude that people had come to be with us.

That night we held our service outdoors on the front porch of the auto mart. We ended the message and started a victory march all around the property. Just as we rounded the last section of pavement, a terrific thunderstorm broke loose pouring rain in torrents. I rejoiced for the Spirit spoke inside of me, "I am going to pour My Spirit on this church."

Out of Space in Five Months

The church took off in the former car dealership location. It was a novelty that caught the news, but more important, it was God's timing in the Spirit. Even with a larger auditorium that seated more people, we were out of space by August.

We decided to purchase a tent seating 1,700 people and pitch it on the parking lot for two morning services. It worked well for two or three months, but in November the rain and cold weather of Oklahoma drove us back inside.

Because of all the remodeling expenses and the monthly payments we were making on the building, we ran into very difficult financial times by the end of 1981. We were paying 15 percent interest on a $3.3 million property. The bills looked so big that we began to face negative thoughts about our future. It was a daily battle just to believe we would survive as a church.

Our family, our life, our personal belongings

were represented on the note we had signed. I knew the power of intimidation of bankers, and I felt the weight of that. After only a few months, I began to pray for deliverance. We were in bondage to the debt on the property. Victory Christian School and Victory Bible Institute did not have room to operate effectively. Plus, the lack of space on Sundays was reaching a point where we were in danger of losing people who needed ministry.

One Sunday we had packed all the people we could in both morning services when a family arrived just a little late with an unsaved friend. Because of the fire marshall's directives, our ushers had to tell them there was no more room. I didn't even know it happened until later that week the family let me know how hard they had worked to get this unsaved friend just to come.

The pain of that conversation was multiplied when we realized there were many others who would be turned away in the weeks ahead. Something had to happen but in the natural there was no solution. Then the Holy Spirit told me to give something away.

CHAPTER NINE

PLANTING A SEED

We prepared to sell the tent we had used for several months. It had become too cold to hold Sunday morning services outside in the tent, so we had moved back into the building and held multiple services.

The Lord spoke to me, "Don't sell the tent. Give it away." That didn't make a lot of sense in the natural because of our financial need, but I knew I had heard from God.

We exchanged the tent for two smaller tents at

the request of Jim Zirkle's Living Water Teaching Ministry in Guatemala, and planted them into his ministry. We were down under financially, but we took what was in our hand and slung it at the giant of debt.

The Bible compares our financial giving to a farmer planting seed. (2 Cor. 9:6-11.) The measure we use to sow will be the measure God uses to return our harvest. Giving flows out of loving God and people. Every time we give in response to the love of God, we release the power of God to work in our own lives.

Seeds multiply. Everything we plant in faith as an act of love will come back to us in some way in due time. Knowing this, we can target our faith and release it through the deliberate act of obedience to the love of God.

One of the greatest harvests from that giving is that those two tents are still being used to win souls on the mission field in Central America.

A month later at our annual Victory Bible Institute Christmas banquet, I had an astounding vision. While Sharon was singing, I was sitting nearby trying to think what I would say to the students. My thoughts were on all our financial needs and on possible reductions of ministries in the church.

As I looked down, I saw an open vision of our church meeting in the ORU Mabee Center, a 10,500-seat multi-purpose sports arena on campus. It was as clear as a television picture before my eyes. Then I heard the voice of God saying the church would be meeting in the Mabee Center

That night when I told Sharon of the vision and the word I had heard, she said, "That'll be a miracle."

She was right. In the natural it was impossible. We were just two of six thousand people who had attended ORU. We had no personal contacts with any of the Roberts' family, regents or leadership of the school. Furthermore, at that time ORU had a standing policy of no church on campus.

Even after the supernatural vision and word, we had no idea or direction on making contact with ORU. However, when something is of God, He works out the details.

God is able to work out the details on His plans without any problem. If a direction is of the Lord, we will see confirming signs and indications pointing that way. Romans 8:28 says: "All things work together for good to them that love God, to them who are the called according to his purpose."

In January we received an invitation to speak at an ORU executive Valentine banquet. The ORU women's club sponsored this annual event for all the deans, administrators and leaders of the university; for Oral Roberts Ministries; and for the City of Faith. They wanted Sharon to sing and me to bring a short message on the theme of Valentine's Day.

The afternoon of the banquet I was in my office praying when it felt as if God dropped a bomb in my lap. It was a strong prophetic word that I was to give at the banquet. The Lord revealed how there were those in leadership who, with strife in their hearts, had spoken against Oral and Evelyn Roberts. The Lord said He would hold them accountable for what they whispered in their bedrooms, and He was removing them from their positions.

I knew it was God's Word for the moment. A boldness came into my spirit that removed all fear.

Something inside told me to take our sound man to the banquet and record the message.

As Sharon and I walked up the sidewalk to ORU that evening, I said to her, "This message will go all over this campus." I had no natural idea how, but I knew it in my heart.

Sharon sang some beautiful love songs and got everyone in a happy, peaceful mood. I sat thinking, "They don't know what is about to happen." I rose to my feet, took the podium and said, "I have a word from God for you."

As I began to speak that God was going to judge them for their strife and rebellion, no one moved. I told them that people cannot touch God's anointed without facing God's discipline. God had instructed me to say that some of them had spoken wrong words and that they would be removed.

I hadn't thought about how to conclude because it wasn't a sermon. I just stopped after I finished saying what God gave me. No one was assigned to dismiss. It was a strange Valentine banquet — people gradually just started getting up to leave.

One of the key leaders ran up to me and said, "You were right on target. Could I get a copy of the tape?"

We sent him a copy the next day and he took it to Oral and Evelyn who had not attended. I learned later they wept as they heard me say how the two of them had paid a price people could not understand.

The Next Step

About six months before the Valentine banquet, I

had mailed an invitation to Oral Roberts to come and preach at our church. He did not travel to churches at that time, but I had heard he had recently gone to one. But we didn't get any response.

A month after the Valentine banquet I was sitting in my office when my secretary said, "Oral Roberts is on the phone for you." At this time I did not know he had listened to my taped message and had it transcribed and printed for every ministry employee.

As I picked up the phone he said, "Could you use me to preach this Sunday?"

Of course I said yes, trying to think quickly which service to give him.

When we called back to tell his secretary that he was scheduled to preach in the 11:00 o'clock Sunday service, we asked what we should do about lunch. She responded that dinner in our home would be fine. I still remember how much work we got done on our yard that Saturday and how much cleaning took place inside. We trimmed the hedge so short it looked barren, so we got the green branches we cut off and stuck them back in the bushes for the weekend!

Brother Roberts' sermon and the time we spent together that Sunday were wonderful. In fact, Oral and Evelyn stayed at our home until after 5:00 talking until Evelyn said, "Oral, let Billy Joe go. He has a church service at 6:00." Somehow I made it on time.

After that weekend, we marveled at God's ability to bring us into favor with the Roberts. Yet, there was no mention of the Mabee Center or our need for larger facilities. We just had to trust that God was working in every step.

Easter Celebration

Several churches decided to unite for a joint Sunday night Easter service in 1982 at the Mabee Center. This was just a month after Brother Roberts had spoken at our church.

He attended the special event and asked to meet with all the pastors afterwards. He poured out his heart concerning his ministry and desire to do God's will. At the end of the fellowship time, he said, "I wish Mabee Center could be used like this every week."

I waited until everyone left and approached Oral with the idea of Victory Christian Center meeting in the Mabee Center, without mentioning my vision. Several days later, he called indicating his desire to see Victory's services conducted in the arena.

Our first service at the Mabee Center was in August 1982, and the vision I had seen nine months before became a reality.

As God gives a vision, He moves people and circumstances to bring it to pass. Yet at the same time we must act in response to His leading to do the things He tells us to do. For our dreams and visions to be fulfilled we must have corresponding actions. Real faith is evidenced by simple obedience.

God revealed to me that our giving of the tent was the seed for the harvest of the Mabee Center. We gave what we had, and God released what we needed.

God had solved our space problem, but we were still in serious bondage to the debt. I had to learn some battle strategy from a shepherd boy named David.

CHAPTER TEN

DAVID'S STRENGTH

I had heard a lot of people preach about David and Goliath, but the Lord brought that story alive to me in a new way. Just like David, we were facing a giant: a giant of debt. I began to ask, "Lord, what did he do to defeat the giant he was facing?"

I saw that Goliath and our debt were no different. They were separated by about three thousand years, but the issues are all the same. Neither David nor I could overcome our giants in our own strength. It was obvious to us and it was obvious to those around us.

I began to pray, and I saw some things about David.

1. David had a relationship with God.

He was a friend of God. He knew Him. He talked with Him. He spent time with Him. When the giant came and wanted to put everybody in bondage, something inside of David rose up and said, "I will not be a slave to a man. I have only one God who will be over me and that is Jehovah."

When you get that kind of conviction inside you, something will begin to rise up and say, "I will not be in bondage to any man."

2. David understood God's covenant.

David understood that God was wholly and completely committed to those who loved and feared Him. That meant everything God had and everything He was would be available to the one with whom He was in covenant. That's why it struck David with such force that nobody stepped forward to challenge Goliath.

When Goliath challenged the nation of Israel, everybody looked at Goliath's size. But David looked at how big God is and said, "What do you mean, challenging the God of the armies of Israel?" David understood that a challenge to him was a direct challenge to Almighty God.

3. David spoke his faith out loud in the face of the lies of the devil.

Goliath told David he would feed his flesh to the

birds of the air and beasts of the field Do you know what David shouted back at him? "Hey! First I'm going to kill you, cut off your head and feed *your whole army* to the birds."

David knew the battle belonged to the Lord and that He would bring a victory David could not accomplish in his own strength. There was not a sword in David's hand. There was a sword in his mouth, the Word of the living God Almighty.

Faith has a language all its own. The ring of authority can be heard in hell when the Word of God is inside your spirit and you speak it out in faith. The devil knows and understands that you know who you are. That's why the devil left Jesus. He spoke with authority. It's time to be fully persuaded that what God has promised, He is able to perform.

Paul wrote, "The word is nigh thee, even in thy mouth, and in thy heart: that is, the word of faith, which we preach" (Rom. 10:8).

4. David learned how to battle the giant by first fighting the lion and then the bear.

David told Saul that before he came to the battle site he was "tending my father's sheep." Now that's a very humbling thing. His older brother said, "Why did you leave those few sheep?" So we know it wasn't some great flock. A few. He was just doing his daily job, doing what he was required to do, but he said, "When a lion came, I took it and I smote it. I destroyed it. When a bear came, I took it with my hands and I destroyed it. And this Philistine will be just like the lion and the bear" (see 1 Sam. 17).

Suddenly it hit me. I was trying to take on the

giant, but I had never fought the lion and the bear. The Lord showed me that what David learned fighting the lion prepared him to fight the bear. What he learned fighting the bear prepared him to fight the giant. There were people in the army of Israel who had never defeated their lion, so when the giant came, they were terrified.

I said, "Well, Lord, here we are. This is the situation." We had literally outgrown the building and parking lot within five months. We were out of space for our school, which had grown to several hundred students. We had no place to grow, no place to go, and a yoke of debt weighing us down.

The Lord gave me a word about the lion, the bear and the giant. "Your lion will be to get an interim site for the schools and offices, a place where you can move to and rent for a temporary time. Your bear will be to sell this building." And then it came like a flash: "Your giant will be to buy land with cash and to build a building debt-free on a cash basis."

I knew that was a real giant.

CHAPTER ELEVEN

THE LION, THE BEAR AND THE GIANT

Our schools were meeting in the auto mart, which we desperately wanted to sell. In 1984 the Lord let me know that the auto mart would sell in the upcoming 1984-85 school year, and we needed to move the school so we wouldn't lose the ministry we had. That would mean double payments, but we just believed the auto mart would sell quickly after we moved to an interim site.

God spoke to me about leasing Thoreau Junior

High, a nearby ten-year-old public school building vacated due to declining enrollment. It was in a prime location, sitting on twenty acres with athletic fields, two gyms, an auditorium, cafeteria, swimming pool, science labs and classrooms. It seemed to be "just right" at that time for our Christian school and Bible institute students, plus ministry offices.

In the spring of 1984 I approached the superintendent three times about leasing the school, but he wanted to sell it for $7 million. We did not want to buy it at that price and limit the ministry to that size of a facility.

I decided to go to the school board meeting in June and ask them for the right to lease the school. Since any citizen has the right to speak if registered on the agenda, I was able to present our case to the entire school board. The superintendent responded publicly to me in the same manner as in our personal contacts: request denied!

The newspaper and TV stations carried the story, and I felt totally rejected. That summer I spent lots of time walking and praying in the early and late hours of the day. A vacant one hundred-acre field adjacent to our home provided a prayer grounds for my hours of searching.

The Holy Spirit clearly impressed me to go after the junior high as our next site, but it was obvious we were not wanted as renters. I was stuck in the middle between God and a school board.

In July the Lord said, "Go back and make them an offer to lease the junior high again." I obeyed and showed up for the monthly meeting. Following my presentation, the superintendent very briefly said, "We have already dealt with this. Next."

I quietly left the board meeting in a state of disappointment and confusion. I was disappointed in my fifth rejection and confused as to why the Lord would send me back.

The next few days as I walked and prayed, it became clear we must do something. Our building had been up for sale for two years and the Holy Spirit confirmed to me it would sell in the next school year. I had no choice but to go back to the school board in August and offer to pay a higher rent.

As I presented a higher offer to the school board, they took a few minutes to discuss their reasons for wanting to sell the building. They said to lease it to us might keep some possible buyer from making an offer.

Each rejection was reported by the television stations and newspaper. It was one of the lowest points in my life and ministry. It appeared we were trapped in a debt situation. We were facing a real lion! The devil was seeking to devour our ministry.

For all practical purposes it appeared the Thoreau door was closed. I tried to relax and rest in Jesus. I found peace in my relationship with Him and rolled the care of our situation onto His shoulders.

The Bible says, "Casting all your care upon him; for he careth for you" (1 Pet. 5:7). To worry and fret is evidence that we have not given God the situation in our heart and mind. Fear is often disguised in the words *deeply concerned*

Jesus cares for us more than we care for ourselves. He has the help we need in every area of our existence As we ask for His help and begin to thank Him in faith, we are rolling our cares upon the Lord.

On Labor Day weekend, Sharon and I decided to go out of town Friday evening with the family before school started on Tuesday. Just as I was stepping into the van, the idea struck me to make one more offer to the school system and give it to the chairman of the board, who had a construction office down the street. We simply offered a higher rent and left it in God's hands.

Returning home Saturday afternoon, I heard from our administrator that the offer was agreeable to the superintendent. The board would accept it at their Tuesday night meeting if we could deliver $120,000 covering the first two and last two months of rent before the meeting started.

On Sunday I made the surprise announcement and our people gave nearly $60,000 to secure the building. That afternoon we received a call from a lady who had visited our church that morning for the first time. She inquired about the amount yet needed to meet the costs by Tuesday and wrote the church a check for the balance!

On Tuesday the cold, unyielding board members I had faced in June, July and August were shaking my hand and slapping me on the back like I was an old friend.

We signed the contract and moved our entire ministry the next Saturday. By Monday, we were conducting school·in Thoreau Junior High for the glory of God.

It took a total of seven approaches to lease the school. In fighting our lion I learned never to give up Just because the door looks closed doesn't mean it's not God leading. Keep persevering, pressing, knocking and doing all you know to do. If it doesn't work one way, try it another way.

The key in persistence is knowing the voice of the Holy Spirit. Some people persistently pursue a wrong direction. If you know God's voice, He will tell you when to keep going, and He will also give you the grace to face the obstacle until the victory is won.

Each time I went back in prayer after being rejected, God would reassure me to try again. My persistence was not outstanding determination within me, but simple obedience to the Father. The bottom line is to do His will.

Our Bear

Our bear was to sell the remodeled auto mart that we had just vacated. When we moved to Thoreau Junior High in September 1984, we were making double monthly payments: $42,000 on the mortgage we still held on the auto mart, and $30,000 on the facility we had just leased, for a total of $72,000 a month.

We had been trying to sell the remodeled auto mart for over two years, but there wasn't one single nibble! It takes a revelation from God to see yourself in remodeled mechanic bays! We had a breezeway where you could punch a button and all the doors opened up. We also had showroom windows — full of glass from floor to ceiling — where we let the light of Jesus shine to passersby through Sunday school and Victory Bible Institute classes.

In November 1984, two months after moving into

the school, we received our one and only call about a buyer for the 4400 South Sheridan property. I learned God can touch anyone He wants at any time in any place.

Sam Walton, one of the richest men in the world, purchased the site for a Sam's Wholesale Club and paid us more than $3.3 million just for the dirt! They demolished the building to make way for a completely new facility. With the closing in January, 1985, we were completely out of debt. Hallelujah!

Our provision came from a company with which we had no personal contact. From this experience I learned not to get my eyes on any person, group or thing to supply my needs. God alone is my Source. To look to anyone or anything other than God always brings disappointment.

Whipping our bear took place over a process of time. David didn't just step on the scene and whip Goliath in one day. It all started when he was a young boy with a little piece of leather and a stone. He built his skill until the moment God could guide the missile that was in his hand into the right place!

Our Giant

Our giant was to purchase land and build our own facilities — with cash.

Because we had experienced the enslavement of debt, I made a decision and a commitment that we would never borrow another dime in the ministry. I got it down in my own spirit that our buying and building would be done with cash.

One day in 1982 while driving down Lewis Avenue in Tulsa, I saw our facilities in the Spirit, across from the ORU Avenue of Flags. I pulled into the Mabee Center parking lot and sketched what I saw.

I discovered that ORU owned the land, and in talking with Oral Roberts I found out he wasn't interested in selling. I wondered, "Did I miss it?" Yet the vision had been so clear.

Two years went by, and in the meantime we did a land search all over town. I never shared my vision with the land search committee because it seemed I had missed it. In my heart I felt I had heard from God, but in my mind there were questions. At the end of their search, they unanimously said, "We believe we are supposed to be near ORU."

Brother Roberts asked us one day, "Where are you going to put your church?"

I said, "We still feel we are supposed to be near ORU."

Brother Roberts said, "I've been thinking about it lately. I don't feel like I can sell you the land, but I would lease it to you."

In December 1984 he made us an offer to lease the land. At that time I had no peace about building a huge complex on leased land, so I held the lease agreement until March 1985, when the Lord spoke to me while I was in prayer, "Sign the lease, and I will work." One week after signing the lease, we printed and distributed a brochure that announced our plans to build at 7700 South Lewis.

Three weeks later I received a call from Brother Roberts. They were having a challenge with the people managing the hotel across the street from ORU, which was built on land ORU leased to them. The company who ran the hotel violated their lease agreement and took a stand that legally and morally opposed ORU's standards.

Brother Roberts said, "We can't have a situation later on where the church and the university would have a conflict. We've got to get out of the lease. But I am a man of my word. Since you have announced your plans to build to your people, the only thing I know to do is offer to sell you the land."

Well, I didn't get too excited because I knew how much the land was worth. The cost of land around ORU was priced at more than $500,000 an acre.

"We will sell the fifteen acres of land to you for $5 million cash," he told me, "and you cannot borrow. You will have to come up with it now." That's kind of like saying, "You can vote if you can write in Chinese!"

I said, "Let me pray about it." While I prayed, the Lord said, "Make an offer similar to the lease agreement." On the lease agreement we were going to lease the front half of the land with an option on the back half.

I went back and made an offer to buy the frontage land for $3.5 million with an option on the back half at $1.5 million in a few years' time. I asked for seven months — from June 2, 1985, to January 2, 1986 — to come up with the $3.5 million.

Our budget for an entire year wasn't $3.5 million, so we would have to raise $3.5 million on top of our entire budget to keep the ministry going — and do it in seven months. I said to Brother Roberts, "If it happens, it will be God. You will know it is God, I will know it is God, the people will know it is God and God will know it is God!"

Brother Roberts said, "OK, it's a deal."

At that time we had about $700,000 in a restricted land and building fund. Two weeks went by and we weren't moving real fast toward the $3.5 million. As I prayed, I asked, "Lord, what do we do?"

He took me back to the story of David and Goliath. He said, "What did David do?"

I said, "He used what was in his hand."

The Lord asked me, "What's in your hand?"

I said, "What do You mean?"

He said, "What does your church have in its hand? How much money do you have?"

I responded, "We have $700,000." Then it hit me. "You want us to give away $700,000?"

The Lord said, "Yes."

In mid-June 1985, I told our congregation, "We've got $700,000 in the land and building account. The Lord has directed that we plant $700,000 into ministries that are meeting needs we aren't meeting — to the poor and missions. We are going to give away $100,000 a month over the next seven months." It suddenly felt like all the air had been vacuumed out of the room.

We gave $700,000 out of our unrestricted account during the next seven months, June through December. Our faith soared with confidence that God had given us *His plan* for receiving financial miracles. The people were with us in the Spirit.

The money came by people planting seeds of faith week after week. They saw God's vision and took it for their own. From little children to senior citizens, it seemed everyone started giving more than ever.

When we came down to the last month before

the $3.5 million was due, we were still $1 million away from our goal. I said, "Lord, we have done everything we can do."

The Lord spoke inside of me and said, "No, you haven't done everything you can do."

God gave us the idea to go on television the very last night, Thursday, January 2, 1986. Dr. Lester Sumrall gave us time on his TV station. By 6:00 that last night we had approximately $300,000 left to raise to meet our midnight deadline. If we didn't meet it with the full $3.5 million, ORU was free from the obligation to sell us the land. At that time they wanted to keep the ownership of the land.

At a quarter before midnight, we were still slightly short of what we needed. We had agreed to meet ORU's administrator at his house at midnight and give him the check. We had a blank check with us. As we headed toward the administrator's house, we stopped at a gas station and called Mike McCutchin, our financial director.

"Mike," I said, "do we have the money?"

He said, "You can write the check!"

Our giant was whipped! We delivered $3.5 million at the moment it was due. God was right on time!

God knows about killing giants. When Adam and Eve fell as a result of rebellion against His commands, the giant of sin came in and said, "I am going to make all of mankind my slaves." God looked around at what He had. He put His only Son in the sling of faith and hurled Him to Calvary!

That single Stone brought down the giants of the devil: sin, sickness, poverty and spiritual death. Today we are no longer slaves to sin, but in Christ we rule and reign in this life because Jesus gave His blood for us. That blood was the price Jesus paid for us. He wanted you and me more than His own life.

First Peter 1:18-19 says:

> Forasmuch as ye know that ye were not redeemed with corruptible things, as silver and gold, from your vain conversation received by tradition from your fathers;
> But with the precious blood of Christ, as of a lamb without blemish and without spot.

As you put your faith in the blood, you can stop the devil's works. The blood is the legal payment for our lives. When we declare what the blood has done for us, the devil is driven back.

> And they overcame him by the blood of the Lamb, and by the word of their testimony (Rev. 12:11).

Building Debt-Free

Just as God had directed, we began building on a cash basis in 1987. The building was designed to be built in phases. The first phase of 125,000 square feet cost more than $7 million. In 1989 we moved in and vacated Thoreau Junior High even though the new building was not fully completed.

The battle to build with cash was very difficult. We had to slow down the work several times as the finances went up and down. But the great thrill was knowing that everything constructed was paid for, and we would not have to pay on it for the next twenty years.

I learned many things about being led by the Spirit from our experiences with the church's property and buildings. I also learned important lessons from something that could have been a terrible personal tragedy for me and my family.

CHAPTER TWELVE

DELIVERED FROM THE FIRE

In 1991 I conducted a funeral for three precious children from our congregation. They had died when a space heater in their home had caught on fire and their old frame house just went up in flames. The mother and father had suffered terrible burns and were grieving deeply.

After that I had an urge in my spirit to buy smoke detectors for our own home. It took about three or four weeks, but finally I went out and bought them. I thought, "I'll put them up later." That was in January.

I put them away and about five months went by until summer.

The thought kept coming back to me: You need to get those smoke detectors up. Finally, one day I got the batteries and put them in.

Later I had a few extra minutes to install the smoke detectors, and I thought, "Well, let's put them up on a good, high spot." I was going to install them on the ceiling, but I couldn't reach high enough and we didn't have a ladder. So I just put the things back on the shelf and forgot about them.

On Monday night, October 21, I went to sleep at approximately 11:00. Sharon stayed up in the den reading till nearly 1:00 before she turned out the lights and went to bed. My back was hurting that night, so I went into the guest bedroom to sleep on a firmer bed.

Because I was not in my bed, Sarah, our oldest daughter, decided to sleep in the room with Sharon. Sarah's room was located in the back of the house in the remodeled garage. Our three other children — Ruth, 11; John, 7; and Paul, 6 — were asleep in their own rooms

Just after 2:00 A.M. I began to hear a beeping sound that resembled Ruthie's alarm clock. The sound was annoying, but it didn't wake me fully. I kept thinking Ruth would get up and shut it off.

As the alarm kept sounding, I finally rolled over to get up and go shut it off. My eyes opened, and as I looked from my bed into the hallway, I could see smoke from the ceiling down to approximately three to four feet off the floor. A night-light in the bathroom revealed how much smoke was in the house

Leaping out of bed, I ran into the hall shouting, "There's a fire! There's a fire! Get out! Get out!" Sharon met me at the opposite end of the hall. She had sat up in bed about the same time I awakened. She thought she was having eye trouble because everything was blurred and dark. The smoke was just above our beds.

We didn't know at this critical moment where the fire was. Being awakened from a sound sleep in the middle of the night makes it difficult to think. By the time we were really awake, the den and the room where Sarah normally slept were in flames. The back corner section of the house had fire breaking through the roof.

I yelled at Sharon to get the kids and I would get the door open. The moment we stood up we were breathing searing hot black smoke filled with carbon monoxide. The super-heated smoke burned my throat and lungs in that first breath. From that point on, I held my breath till we got outside.

Getting the front door open was nearly impossible. The den wall was on fire. Only a couple of layers of drywall was between the fire and the front door. Everything was jet black. The latch was so hot it burned my hand.

After a struggle, it opened, and I pulled back the wooden front door. Next was the glass door. It opened, but then a backdraft started forcing it shut. Hot, black air was rushing outside on the top half while cooler outside air came rushing in the lower half. The fire sucked in the fresh air like a vacuum.

Still unable to breathe, I stood inside the house pushing against the glass door as hard as I could to keep it open. I heard Sharon and the kids coughing and running toward the doorway. I could hear her yelling, "Get out! There's a fire!" I could only hear and feel them as they brushed me on the way out before I followed them onto the sidewalk to our driveway.

They're Still in the House!

The air felt so good when we were out. I looked at the kids but didn't see our eleven-year-old, Ruth. Sharon shouted, "Ruthie's still in there!" Somehow she had lost her way in getting out. It's hard to imagine the feelings of a child awakened in the night with shouts of "There's a fire! Get out!" Ruth had started out of her bedroom door to follow Sharon down the hall but became disoriented in all the confusion.

I ran to the house and pulled the glass door back open. The backdraft was powerful as it sucked air into the full blaze of our den and Sarah's bedroom. The hot black smoke hit my face and for a moment some of it went into my lungs before I remembered not to breathe.

I started down the pitch black, smoke-filled hallway waving my arms trying to locate Ruth. My hand hit her head. Thank You, Jesus. She was standing dazed in the middle of the hallway with no idea which way to go. I grabbed her by the hair and began to pull her back down the hall and then out the door.

The fresh air felt so good to my burning lungs. The fire seemed to gain strength with the extra oxygen from the door opening. I ran into the front yard trying to make sure we had everyone. I saw

Sarah and John and then shouted, "Where's Paul?" Our little six year old had lost his way.

Sharon yelled, "He must still be in the house!"

The door was even harder to open and the smoke was fire hot as I started once again through the entryway and then to the right down the hall. I waved my hands about three feet from the floor feeling for our little six year old. One of the greatest moments of my life was the second my hand touched his little head. I grabbed Paul's pajama top and jerked him into my arms as we ran back down the hall.

Just as we started away from the front door, the windows beside it exploded and flames came leaping out. The fire broke through the roof as we headed to our neighbors. My red pajamas were jet black from my waist up and my face was even darker.

We gathered our family on the front porch of our next-door neighbors, the Browns, and thanked God for saving us. We were watching the flames as the firemen arrived and other neighbors began to walk down the street.

George Brown drove me to the hospital because my breathing was so difficult. The rest of the family was unharmed.

One of the firemen quizzed Sharon, looking for possible clues to the cause of the fire. He said, "Were you burning candles?"

"No," she said. Then he asked, "Were you smoking?"

Sarah was standing beside her and said indignantly, "No!" With the house in flames and me on the way to the hospital, Sharon said, "We don't smoke, we don't chew, and we don't go with girls that do." And then she gave a great big laugh. That was the joy we all felt just to be alive.

We hadn't lost anything that really mattered. In fact, we never grieved a moment over the loss of our material possessions. Our youth pastor, Ray Barnard, said, "Pastor, some of your clothes needed to burn anyway."

Supernatural Prayer Support

Prayer — believing prayer — brings deliverance.

One family in our congregation later shared with us how at 10:30 that night, they gathered for their family prayer time, and the Spirit of God took them into deep intercession for us, weeping and crying out for our deliverance.

I received another letter from a woman who said she was awakened at 2:00 A.M. and prayed for us.

Romans 8:26 says that when we do not know how to pray, the Spirit makes intercession with groanings and utterances which cannot be spoken in our own language. He knows the heart of God. He knows what our needs are, and He will pray in accordance with God's will and in accordance with the need.

Ephesians 6 says that we're to watch always with all prayer and supplication for all the saints.

I thank God for people praying for us so that we were awakened and able to escape death. I thank God we woke up when we did in time to get everybody out of there. I want to encourage you to watch and pray one for another.

God moves in response to the prayer of faith.

Being led by the Spirit in prayer takes us out of a limited world into God's limitless revelation. He put our family on the hearts of people who had no idea what was coming against us.

The fireman who wrote the report on the fire said they came prepared to pull bodies out of the burning house. It was the worst-case scenario for a house fire. The smoke was so hot all through the house, they were amazed anyone survived. After five days of investigation they determined the cause was a wiring problem in a ceiling light.

Thank God we came through! Brother Roberts and Richard gave us the opportunity to rent an ORU staff house until we moved to a different home. Another family built a brand-new house on the lot where our house burned. Every time we think about it, we give thanks to God for delivering us from the fire.

The fire happened exactly one month before our first crusade in Russia. The greatest soul-winning effort of our lives was only days away from that night of deliverance.

CHAPTER THIRTEEN

SEIZING THE MOMENT IN RUSSIA

There are always opportunities that come across our pathway ordained and arranged by God. Many people are not aware, not looking for what God is doing, and they miss opportunities that God has given them.

Not every opportunity comes from God. It takes a spirit sensitive to the Holy Spirit and spending time with God's Word to rightly divide between what God is saying and your own thoughts. Remember, it is the Word that divides between the soul and the spirit. Sometimes people want to do things in the soulish realm, but it is the Holy Spirit that we need to follow. The Word divides between the two.

When you know God has given you a direction, seize the moment. You see, God is interested in timing. I've heard people say that God does not relate to time — that He's outside of time. But I asked myself, "Who originated time?" God did. So obviously, if He created it, it has to be important.

Who thought of day and night? Genesis 1 tells us God did.

Who thought of seasons? It wasn't man's idea to create summer, fall, winter and spring. All of those are demarcations of time that God created, and God is into timing and seasons.

Ecclesiastes puts the whole thing into focus for us and says, "To every thing there is a season, and a time to every purpose under the heaven" (Eccl. 3:1.)

God moves people and things into place in order to fulfill His plans. Remember when Abraham was going up the mountain to offer his son Isaac as a sacrifice? At the same time, God was moving a ram to be caught in a thicket right at the very place where Abraham would be stopped by an angel and God would say, "Don't slay your son, Isaac. Now I know you are a covenant-keeping man."

Abraham would see the ram caught and declare that God is *Jehovah-Jireh,* the God who sees, which we could translate, "the God who sees ahead and makes provision." Or we call it, "God our provider." Why? Because God is into timing. Timing meant everything when God spoke to me about Russia.

Crusades in Russia

As early as 1980 I heard the prophetic word, "God is going to open the door to Russia for the gospel." At times I could see myself preaching to those precious people. Inside, I felt the urge to be a part of the great harvest that would come. The Holy Spirit was preparing me for the time appointed by God when He would call in a great harvest from the former Soviet Union.

In the first part of 1991, the Holy Spirit told us to print one million copies of the book *This New Life* in Russian. I had written it in 1977 as a basic tool to instruct new converts on salvation, the Holy Spirit, faith, righteousness, healing and the abundant life in Jesus. God had let me know from the very beginning that the book would reach people around the world.

Russia was not open to the gospel in the spring of 1991, but I was compelled to get the books printed in Russian and ready for distribution. Dennis Lindsay coordinated the project in Russia, and it finally took a train boxcar of beef in exchange for paper to get the printing started in Minsk, Russia. By the summer we had most of the books printed but had no major outlets for their distribution.

That summer Sharon and I went to South Bend, Indiana, to preach for Dr. Lester Sumrall at his June camp meeting. Before introducing us, he talked of his plans to conduct an August ministry crusade in St. Petersburg, Russia. The Holy Spirit spoke to me that I was to go be a part of that team.

After the service we went back to a fellowship dinner for all the ministers in attendance. Sitting down by Dr. Sumrall, I said, "So you're going to Russia."

He whirled around to face me and said bluntly, "Yeah, why don't you go with me?"

I said, "I'll do it," and it was settled.

The Vision

Just ten days before the crusade in late August 1991, Gorbachev was abducted and a coup attempt took place. We had no idea this would signal the collapse of the Soviet Union, thus opening the door to all the communist republics. History was being made in those very hours.

As a result of the coup, most of the planned advertising for our crusade was stopped, causing the crowds to be smaller than we anticipated. Six to eight thousand attended our services in a huge sports complex capable of seating up to twenty-five thousand people. The good news was that every altar call brought crowds of people giving their lives to Jesus Christ.

We had Russian *This New Life* books to give to all who attended. Immediately the people had the simple teaching of God's Word to help them get established in the faith. In fact, this was the primary literature available at that crusade. Praise God for the leading of the Spirit to print it earlier that year.

As I stood at one of those altar calls, in my spirit I saw the arena seats filled with people. I had this immediate impression in my mind and heart that we were to return for another crusade very soon. Before leaving for America, we arranged a potential date in November to come back for a large meeting.

As soon as I arrived back in Tulsa, we announced our plans to the church.

We attempted to coordinate our plans through the people in Russia who had helped Dr. Sumrall. However, they felt it would be better to wait until the following summer for another major crusade. For two weeks we called and sent messages back and forth until they made it clear their organization could not help us.

We received their response on a Monday in September 1991. I had thought I was hearing from the Lord, but with this response every indication was negative. There was no way to do a crusade in St. Petersburg at that time without help from strong people who lived in that city. We didn't know anyone else capable of undertaking the project. With a sense of defeat, I took the file of information on Russia and put it away. It seemed to be over.

Thank God for the Holy Spirit. All week long I kept thinking about the people, sensing the door to Russia would only be open a brief time. Many prophetic words revealed the harvest would be quick and then the door would close. At the moment it already seemed to be closed for us, but the Holy Spirit kept flooding me with compassion for the people.

When the Holy Spirit is leading you to do something, the thought of it continues to come up into your mind from your spirit. Also, there is a witness of a strong urging deep within you to do what God is speaking.

I knew there was no peace in me concerning dropping the November '91 Russia crusade, yet in my mind I did not know what to do. The strong leading to go to Russia would not leave me.

It grew in me all week long. Sunday morning as I was tying my shoes to get ready for services, I spoke out, "We are going in November." Faith welled up inside me, and I knew God would work things out.

After preaching and ministering that Sunday, I went to the back of the Mabee Center to greet people. Three men and a woman I had never seen walked up to me and said in broken English, "We hear you are going to Russia. We are from St. Petersburg and want to help you." The men were pastors, and the woman was the wife of one of them.

Someone had heard my announcement three weeks before and told these Russians who had come to Tulsa. They had all the contacts necessary to help make the crusade happen. God knew what He was doing all along. He is *Jehovah-Jireh,* the Lord who provides.

Crusade Coordinators

Another amazing part of God's plan was a couple who moved to Tulsa from Cleveland, Tennessee, just to volunteer in our church. Nic Porter was an engineer and both he and his wife, Mary, were very capable, hard workers.

After our book *This New Life,* got into the hands of thousands of Russians, we began to receive letters from them. When I asked our staff for ideas on how to handle the mail, one said, "Nic Porter speaks and reads Russian. He probably could handle them."

Not only did Nic handle it, but he and Mary moved to St. Petersburg that fall to coordinate all of our crusades in those first months. The miracle was that God had spoken to them to come to Tulsa, but they didn't know why. Without any children and free from any long-term house payments or an apartment lease, they were in a position to move to Russia immediately. Since Nic knew the language, they had no problem adjusting to the culture and helping us get ready for the November crusade.

Surprise! Eighteen Months

The first Russian crusade was life-changing for Sharon and me. We saw what could happen in a country ready for the gospel. In those seven services, 25,584 people gave their lives to Jesus.

The Lord spoke to me after the very first service from Acts 18:9-11. As I was directed by the Holy Spirit to turn to this passage, it was clear Jesus was speaking.

> Be not afraid, but speak, and hold not thy peace: For I am with thee, and no man shall set on thee to hurt thee: for I have much people in this city. And he continued there a year and six months, teaching the word of God among them.

The Lord clearly spoke to me to hold crusades for eighteen months in St. Petersburg teaching the Bible. It was a confirmation of the word I had received on the return flight from the August crusade.

> For thus saith the Lord God, My people went down aforetime into Egypt to so-

journ there; and the Assyrian oppressed them without cause (Is. 52:4).

The Russian people had been oppressed by the communists who ruled the nation.

Now therefore, what have I here, saith the Lord, that my people is taken away for nought? they that rule over them make them to howl, saith the Lord; and my name continually every day is blasphemed (Is. 52:5).

Atheism in Russia denounced the name of the Lord daily from the elementary schools to the university classrooms. The common people were like slaves working for the good of the state.

Therefore my people shall know my name: therefore they shall know in that day that I am he that doth speak: behold, it is I (Is. 52:6).

God promised to reveal Himself to these desperate, suffering people. My question was, "What was my part in this harvest?" When I read these first three verses, God opened my eyes to see His view of the Russian people. Then came God's direction.

How beautiful upon the mountains are the feet of him that bringeth good tidings, that publisheth peace; that bringeth glad tidings of good, that publisheth salvation; that saith unto Zion, Thy God reigneth! (Is. 52:7).

It was clear we were to go with the good news.

It Happened!

The January 1992 crusade took us all by surprise. The Russian people were filled with fear about the future. Boris Yeltsin had just come to power and no one knew what would happen. There was little food or Western aid coming into the nation. It looked as if millions of Russians might starve before the winter was over.

We announced the crusade through the media, and we had a supply of New Testaments on hand for those who would be attending the services.

We were in God's timing. More than thirteen thousand attended the first night. During the next three days we saw eighteen thousand to twenty-one thousand people in each of the six services.

We used commitment cards for the first fifty thousand decisions, then we ran out. Based on the attendance in the final services and first-time responses, a total of more than ninety-six thousand people responded to the altar calls. Everyone attending received a New Testament and a copy of *This New Life.*

Sharon and I stood in awe as we watched the people run to the altar by the thousands. The vision I had seen at age eighteen of the two of us preaching and ministering to masses of people was being fulfilled before our eyes twenty-one years later.

Miraculous Strength

The eighteen months of crusades were miraculous. First of all, our ability to preach in Tulsa on Sunday, fly to Russia on Monday and Tuesday, preach seven services Tuesday through Friday, board a plane on Saturday and fly back to Tulsa in one day and preach the next day in two Sunday morning services was supernatural. We did this sixteen times during those eighteen months. Only twice did we get stuck an extra day in Finland on our return trip to America due to snowstorms

We were in awe at the energy and strength God gave us in addition to an overflowing joy of the Lord. The same Spirit that raised Jesus from the dead was quickening our mortal bodies (Rom. 8:11).

My mom had moved to Tulsa a few years before to help us in the administration of the church. As we went to Russia, she was there to be with our children and ensure they had the love and help they needed. Praise God she heard and obeyed the voice of the Holy Spirit calling her to leave a place she had lived for almost forty years.

In June God brought Terry and Brenda Henshaw to lead the founding of Victory Christian Center and Bible Institute in St. Petersburg, Russia. It had taken only a few months to realize the need for training Russians to start churches and do the work of the ministry. We felt the work of equipping believers in an in-depth school could have just as much long-term impact as the crusades.

Today there are Americans and Russians working side by side in what was formerly Leningrad, with outreach ministries going into other parts of Russia.

Through the crusades and Victory Christian Cen ter and Victory Bible Institute in St. Petersburg, over

3.3 million pieces of literature have been distributed: 1 million New Testaments; 3,000 complete Bibles; 1.6 million *This New Life* books; and 574,400 illustrated children's books. The greatest harvest is yet to come as these seeds grow and multiply.

Fill Your Sails

God gives windows of opportunity, but if you're not sensitive in your spirit and you have your own agenda, you'll go right on with your program and miss the supernatural program of God

There's a moment to act, and when you do, it's like catching a wave that you ride all the way to the shore. It's like catching the wind in a sail — if you get your sail up at the right time and you are in the right place to catch the wind, it will carry you all the way to your goal.

We realized we were in the right place at the right time in Russia. The amazing harvest of those crusades was not due to our great ability, but rather to our availability to do His will. The Russian people didn't know us, but we were there when they were desperate and ready to come and hear about Jesus.

To try and do the right thing at the wrong time is always frustrating. But, oh, the joy of being at the right place, with the right message, before the right people in the *right time!*

CHAPTER FOURTEEN

DESIRING TO BE LED

You may be thinking, I understand you have heard from God, but I don't know if I've ever been led by the Spirit of God. If you have been saved, you have been led by the Spirit. It was not the devil that led you to be saved. It was not even yourself. Unless God draws a person and works inside of his or her heart, they cannot be saved. Jesus said, "No man can come to me, except the Father which hath sent me draw him" (John 6:44).

Your salvation experience was the greatest leading of God's Spirit that you will ever experience in your life. If you have not been saved, it is certainly God's Spirit that led you to read this book. You can confess Jesus as Lord right now and ask Him to fill you with His Spirit. Go ahead and do it.

Everything flows out of following that leading to believe that Jesus Christ came in the flesh as the Son of God, that He bled and died and suffered for our sins, that He was buried and rose from the dead. Today, whoever will call upon Him as Lord and Savior, the Scriptures say, will be saved.

It is the Word of God that comes inside our minds and illumines our thinking and reveals to us that Jesus Christ is the Son of God. That's a work of the Holy Spirit in your life.

I want to affirm to you that the Holy Spirit has worked in your life and desires to do more.

The Bible says you *are* led by the Spirit of God. Remember, sons of God are led by the Spirit of God (Rom. 8:14). Jesus tells us that He is the good Shepherd. His sheep hear His voice. A stranger they will not follow (see John 10). You are one of God's sheep.

Begin to believe. Declare it with your lips. Say out loud, "I am led by the Spirit of God. I do hear God's voice. I won't follow the voice of a stranger."

God wants you to know His will even more than you want to know it.

Think about how the Holy Spirit inspired the writing of the Bible through many centuries and many authors. Why? So that we would know the will of God through the ages and the revelation of that will through His Son Jesus.

111

False Leading

Christians are so privileged to be led by the Holy Spirit. People who don't know Jesus have to rely on poor substitutes.

The mind

One way people are led is by their own natural thinking. The Apostle Peter, for example, did not think Jesus should go through the crucifixion. He tried to stop Him from doing it. Jesus turned around and rebuked Satan because it was Satan who had inspired that thought in Peter's mind (Mark 8:33).

Peter could not figure out why Jesus should go through with this thing of being crucified, buried and raised from the dead on the third day.

I can recall how, as a college student, I tried to choose a career by taking an aptitude test. Since junior high school I had wanted to be a forest ranger. But my aptitude test said I wasn't inclined to be a forest ranger. The test showed there were many other occupations more suited for me.

I looked at one career and thought, "Well, this other career has lots of openings in it, and you can make a lot of money." That's how a lot of people choose their careers. There is nothing wrong with an aptitude test, but what really matters is getting the Holy Spirit's direction

Five natural senses

Other people are led by their five senses. A man sees a woman and says, "I like what I see. I think I'll marry her." A lot of people make the mistake of getting married based on what they see

People can be fooled by their senses. When Abraham told Lot to take whatever land he wanted, Lot looked down on a beautiful, watered plain, and to him it was obviously the best land. But he ignored something. It was the land of Sodom and Gomorrah. For the sake of some nice land, Lot subjected his family into a lifestyle that literally cost his wife her life (Gen. 13:10-12, 19:26).

Worldly attitude
Instead of being led by the Spirit, some people are led by a worldly attitude; they see life the way the world does. The prodigal son was a young man who was led by a worldly attitude. He figured that at a certain age you get your dad's money and go party and have a good time.

The same worldly attitude exists today: Eat, drink and be merry. Many are caught up and led by it. "That's what everybody is doing," they say. Thank God there is another way to be led.

Spirit Leading

God did give us the five senses, a mind to think, and an understanding of how the universe works so that we can work with the laws of nature

We should not ignore those things when making a decision, but they must be subjected to the Spirit of God. What is God's Spirit saying?

Let's look at three incidents in the book of Acts where people were led by the Spirit.

"Join Yourself to This Chariot"

Philip was preaching a red-hot revival in Samaria (see Acts 8). It was his first big meeting and everything was going great. Crowds were coming, but then God said, "Leave this place and go down to the desert." In the natural thinking it didn't make much sense.

A lot of what God says to you will not make sense to your natural thinking.

Philip went down to the desert and saw a chariot going by with an Ethiopian in it. The Spirit said to Philip, "Go near and join yourself to this chariot."

God is a God of specifics. Do you know the Holy Spirit can tell you which car to buy? If He can tell Philip which chariot to get in, He can tell you which car or house to buy.

Some people say God's not concerned with things like that. Let me ask you something: Where do you make the separation? Where do you draw the line in your life between what God is concerned with and what He's not? Why don't you just believe He's interested in all of it?

Acknowledge Him and let Him speak to you. Proverbs says, "In all thy ways acknowledge him, and he shall direct thy paths" (Prov. 3:6).

Remember when the Lord spoke to me that He was going to open the doors of denominational churches? Later He gave me the month to begin: January, 1976.

God was directing our paths in specific ways.

When we obeyed what the Lord had spoken, the picture He gave me was that of Peter coming out of prison. Wherever Peter walked, the doors opened

114

of their own accord. Sharon and I look back at some of the places we went and realize God miraculously opened doors.

We went to churches where the pastors didn't even want us — and they told us so. But God got hold of their board and the board said, "Bring this guy in."

At one church there was a group of older ladies who heard Sharon sing. They put the pressure on the pastor, and when they said, "We want this couple in our church," we walked through an open door.

God has ways! He told us ahead of time it was going to happen and we just walked through those doors by the leading of the Holy Spirit.

I believe God will tell you which church to attend. Whenever you are led by God to a church, you're going to be with it in giving and receiving. Your life will have impact in it and it will have impact on your life.

God can tell you who to marry. My wife and I know a young woman who went through a horrible marriage that ended in divorce. We asked her about it one day and she said, "Two weeks before that marriage even took place, I felt inside me not to go through with the marriage."

She ended up in a physically abusive situation where her life was in danger. We said, "Why didn't you back out of the wedding instead of going through this horrible experience?"

She said, "I'd already had two showers, and people had given me gifts. I felt it would be an embarrassment to me and a disappointment to them to call it off."

She allowed the suffering in her heart when she

should have let those things in the natural go. God will tell you who to join yourself to in marriage.

"Go With Them"

God told Peter that some Gentiles would call for him at the house where he was staying. In the natural, Peter did not want to go with them, but by the Holy Spirit, God told him what to do.

> While Peter thought on the vision, the Spirit said unto him, Behold, three men seek thee. Arise therefore, and get thee down, and go with them, doubting nothing: for I have sent them (Acts 10:19-20).

For those of you in business: You can tell by the Spirit who God has sent to you. This happened to me when we were in a town in central Arkansas. "Three men are going to come," the Holy Spirit spoke to us through the pastor's wife. "Two men will be lying. One will be telling the truth."

That night in the service it happened, and God had the word for them that they needed to know.

As the three men stood before me, I asked about their situation. Two of them gave an answer that was deceptive. By the Spirit I spoke of the real situation and how they were to yield to God's Spirit. They acknowledged it was correct. The other man spoke truthfully, and we prayed for the need he revealed.

David du Plessis was a classical Pentecostal raised in Pentecostal tradition. All of his life he had heard preaching against Catholics and thought the pope was the Antichrist.

In the 1950s, God spoke to him, "I want you to go and join yourself to the World Council of Churches. I want you to go and minister to the Catholics." David du Plessis wanted to resist that calling, not only because of what his fellow ministers would say, but because of his own background and things he had said.

But du Plessis realized God had spoken to him. He joined the World Council of Churches, and whenever they had questions about the charismatic movement — speaking in tongues or the gifts of the Spirit — they asked David du Plessis to address the council.

He had an opportunity to tell archbishops and bishops of the Catholic church about the moving of the Spirit. He was instrumental in helping to bring about a Catholic charismatic renewal that started in the late 1960s.

In his natural mind, du Plessis was just like Peter. He didn't want to join himself to that group. Sometimes prejudices can be along religious lines. But God told him to go, and he obeyed, and today we see revival and renewal as a result of du Plessis' obedience.

Isaiah 1:19-20 says, "If ye be willing and obedient, ye shall eat the good of the land: But if ye refuse and rebel, ye shall be devoured with the sword." Obedience is the evidence that we believe God's Word. It is the corresponding action in our faith.

"Don't Go"

The Holy Spirit will also stop you from doing things that could harm you or put you out of God's perfect plan. The book of Acts tells of two times when the Holy Spirit stopped Paul from travelling to certain places.

> Now when they had gone throughout Phrygia and the region of Galatia, and were forbidden of the Holy Ghost to preach the word in Asia, after they were come to Mysia, they assayed to go into Bithynia: but the Spirit suffered them not (Acts 16:6-7).

I know a couple, Dick and Betty Mills, who have a strong teaching ministry. Someone presented them with a proposal for a computer system that required a large initial investment of money but seemed to be perfect for what they needed. Dick was all excited about it and turned to his wife and asked, "What do you think, honey?"

The Spirit of God rose up in her and she said, "He's a phony."

It turned out the salesman was a con artist. He didn't even have such a product and was ripping people off up and down the West Coast with a presentation of a false system. The Spirit of God said, "Don't go into it." By God's divine direction, that couple was spared the loss of money and a heartbreaking situation.

Guidance for Every Day

We are living in a day where we need to be led by the Holy Spirit.

When I think about it, this is one of the most

exciting studies and subjects in my whole life —
being led by the Spirit of God, divine guidance,
knowing the will of God. The reason is: I need
guidance continually. I have decisions to make
every day — just like you do.

It is wonderful when I know I am doing the right
thing at the right time, in the right place in the right
way with the right people. That's what it's like to be
led by the Holy Spirit..

There are three simple things you can do to experience the guidance of the Holy Spirit in your life

1. *Desire to be led by the Spirit of God.*

If you want to be led, God wants to lead you.
Desire is the biggest issue. People who refuse to be
led, or don't even think about it, seldom realize the
leading of God's Spirit. Just say, "Lord, I want to be
led. I'm open to it. I desire to be led by Your Spirit."
John 10:27 says:

> My sheep hear my voice, and I know
> them, and they follow me.

When you're choosing different courses to take in
school, why not ask the Lord? Ask Him about career
choices too. Ask Him about that move. Just because
the company tells you to move doesn't mean the
Spirit of God says to move. Or, just because the
company says you're supposed to stay in a certain
place doesn't mean God's Spirit says to stay. Those
things may or may not be the leading of the Lord.

Sometimes God leads through open doors. He
opens doors that no one can shut (Rev. 3:8). He
also shuts doors that no one can open. The key

question is this "What does the Spirit of God say?" Just because there are open doors does not mean you are to walk through them. It may be a trap door or snare that you would walk into. But your spirit will show you which door to walk through if you will acknowledge God.

2. Listen.

Revelation 2:7 says "He that hath an ear, let him hear what the Spirit saith unto the churches " You would think since people had ears, they would listen. So why is this phrase used seven times in Revelation 2 and 3; he who has ears, let him listen? Because it is possible to have ears and still not be listening. God is not talking about natural ears. He's talking about the ears of your heart.

I can look back at mistakes we've made, such as buying a trailer instead of a van, and they happened because we went with another person's opinion instead of what we felt in our spirits. God's grace redeemed us so we were able to sell the trailer and get the van we needed. I went through a lot of regret but I learned to pray in earnest, "Lord, let me be sensitive to Your voice. Let me have a hearing ear."

3. Ask specifically.

James 1:5-8 says, "If any of you lack wisdom, let him ask of God, that giveth to all men liberally and upbraideth not; and it shall be given him. But let him ask in faith, nothing wavering. For he that wavereth is like a wave of the sea driven with the wind and tossed. For let not that man think that he shall receive any thing of the Lord. A doubleminded man is unstable in all his ways." Mark 11:24 declares:

> What things soever ye desire, when ye pray, believe that ye receive them, and ye shall have them.

Be specific in prayer based on the desire God has implanted in your heart. Faith is based on God's Word. Find the scriptures that specifically promise what you are asking.

> If we ask any thing according to his will, he heareth us: And if we know that he hear us, whatsoever we ask, we know that we have the petitions that we desired of him (1 John 5:14-15).

Confidence

Jesus promised that God will answer our cries for the Holy Spirit.

> If a son asks for bread from any father among you, will he give him a stone? Or if he asks for a fish, will he give him a serpent instead of a fish? Or if he asks for an egg, will he offer him a scorpion?
> If you then, being evil, know how to give good gifts to your children, how much more will your heavenly Father give the Holy Spirit to those who ask Him! (Luke 11:11-13, NKJV)

After hearing about the baptism of the Holy Spirit in 1972, I asked in faith and received a wonderful infilling of His presence and power. At that moment I began to speak in a new language of prayer and praise. To this day that flow of the Spirit still comes up from within me in joy, wisdom, revelation, encouragement and strength.

So ask in confidence, with excitement, for you will receive your answer.

CHAPTER FIFTEEN

THE INWARD WITNESS

How is the Spirit of God going to speak to us? We might define or describe the way God speaks to us in many different ways. One person might say, "I have a deep feeling down inside." Another person may say, "I've got a gut feeling." Another just says, "There is something inside of me saying...," "There is a voice I keep hearing" or "There is a thought that just keeps coming back to me."

Colossians 3:15 says, "Let the peace of God rule

in your hearts." There are two key words here: peace and rule. The *peace* of God comes from the Holy Spirit, the Spirit of peace. The Amplified Version says the word *rule* implies "to act as umpire continually." So another way the Holy Spirit helps you umpire or judge things in your life is by means of His peace that you feel in your heart.

The reverse is that the Holy Spirit may also guide you by a lack of peace or a troubled feeling. At times you may sense His warning.

Someone might say, "Well, I've never heard God speak." Have you ever listened? Have you ever purposed to listen?

God is no respecter of persons (Acts 10:34). He speaks to all His children.

Perhaps you can look in retrospect at your life and say, "You know, I was being led by the Spirit of God and didn't even realize it." You would say, "That was just what I felt deep down inside me. People were telling me this, but it looked like I ought to do that. I even had reached a certain conclusion in my mind. But deep down inside I felt a different direction."

That "deep down inside of you" is the Holy Spirit.

Often our minds cannot fully comprehend what the Spirit is saying. That is why we need to listen for the voice of God inside of us.

Paul talked about the "inward man" (2 Cor. 4:16). Peter talked about the "hidden man of the heart" (1 Pet. 3:4). God speaks to your heart, which is another way of saying He speaks to your spirit.

That's why Proverbs 3:5 says, "Trust in the Lord with all thine heart." In your heart is where you feel the inward witness of your spirit.

Hindrances to Hearing

Why don't people listen to their spirits more so they can experience more supernatural interventions?

Thorns

In the parable of the sower, Jesus said God's Word can be choked out by thorns. Thorns represent three things: the cares of this world, the deceitfulness of riches, and the lusts for other things (Mark 4:19).

Cares of life are the duties people carry out in the process of living, such as jobs, caring for families and other obligations. These things are good, but people let them consume their lives until God's wonderful opportunities, protection, direction, deliverance, empowering, preservation and purifying are bypassed because they are too busy doing other things.

To be consumed with getting money, spending money and keeping money in place of seeking and knowing God is the deceitfulness of riches. The deceitfulness of riches can choke out spiritual sensitivity for both rich and poor people. It's not a matter of how much you have, but placing too much priority on material things.

Then there is the lust for other things. Some people worship the god of activity. Our society is consumed with recreation, hobbies, projects and causes that can keep people on a constant treadmill. Pursuing things instead of God causes the Word to be neglected and thus non-productive in a person's life.

Other voices

Too many other voices can crowd out the voice of the Holy Spirit. What do I mean by other voices? I'm talking about radio, TV, newspaper, videos, magazines, CDs and cassettes that contradict the voice of the Lord. Things that are not in line with God's voice in our spirits can create confusion, distortion and deception.

People say, "Well, the things I'm letting into my life are not saying anything about God either way." But if so much of your heart and mind is filled with them, it's hard to distinguish God's voice in the midst of it all.

Sometimes we listen so much to the opinions of other people that we dull our sensitivity to what God is saying to us. I can look back on some occasions in my life where I missed the Spirit's voice because I was affected by the opinions of others.

Pride

Another reason why people do not listen to their spirit is because of pride. They are proud of their own opinions, intellect, background, education and accomplishments. So they don't acknowledge God.

God has said many times in Scripture that pride always comes before a fall. Samson is an example. I believe his spirit told him repeatedly, "Don't go down into the region of the Philistines." But he was too proud to listen and eventually fell. He ended up a blind man grinding grain like an ox. The glory and the power he had known were lost.

Though God used the end of Samson's life to accomplish a great victory, there was also great sorrow during the years he served as a slave to the Philistines.

We can't run our own lives. But if we trust in the Lord with all our heart and acknowledge Him in all our ways, He will direct our paths.

The humble person says, "God help me. Direct me, lead me, guide me, show me. What is it? What are you saying?" God resists the proud but gives grace to the humble.

Lies

Many times people shut out the voice of their spirit because they have been fed lies for so long they can't even tell what the truth is. One of the biggest problems in America right now is the humanistic education system. The deception that we evolved from monkeys and there is no such thing as God creating the world has sent millions to hell.

Have you ever wondered how supposedly sensible, intelligent men and women who have been trained as judges and lawyers could say abortion should be allowed at the choice of the mother? They want it to be legal to take a helpless unborn baby who has a heartbeat, fingers, arms and legs and literally rip that baby apart while it is in the mother's womb. That is insanity. It's not even human that a person would treat a baby like that.

How do you get people to that point? You feed them humanistic education over a long process of time. You keep telling them a lie long enough until they believe it. You say, "That's not really a person. That's a fetus — just a mass of flesh." You keep telling them that every individual has the right to choose what they want to do with their life regardless of others. You keep teaching situational ethics — the situation determines the rules You say there is no right and wrong.

If you educate people like that from the first grade through the twelfth grade and into college, they get to the point where they literally believe with all their hearts that what they are doing is right. According to the input they have had in their lives, their minds say that they are right. They can literally look at what is wrong and call it right.

Staying Sensitive to the Spirit

Now that we've examined hindrances to hearing the inward witness of the Holy Spirit, let's take a look at ways we can encourage our spirits to remain sensitive to His leading.

Immerse your spirit in the things of God

As you feed your spirit with the things of God, you become more sensitive to His guidance. As time passes you can learn to let God guide you in the smallest details of your life.

Commune with the Holy Spirit

As you pray and spend time alone with Him — an extended period of time on a daily basis — you become accustomed to His voice. You can sense it, know it and recognize it. You are aware of it.

If you don't spend time with Him, you won't be able to discern His voice when He speaks to you. You'll think, Is that what my mother said? Is that what I heard at the pizza shop? Is that what I heard on the radio? Or is that what the Spirit is saying?

Read God's Word

Develop a consistent pattern of Scripture reading. Take time to be in places where God's Word is being preached with the anointing of the Holy Spirit.

Worship and Praise

Spend time in places where prayer, worship and praise are used to take authority over the things that are not of God. Praise invites God's presence. God inhabits the praises of His people (Ps. 22:3). At the same time praise is a weapon against the enemy (Ps. 149). It drives out darkness and breaks the oppression of the devil. Matthew 21:16 says:

> Out of the mouth of babes and sucklings
> thou hast perfected praise.

This is a quote from Psalm 8:2 which says, "Out of the mouth of babes and sucklings hast thou ordained strength because of thine enemies, that thou mightest still the enemy and the avenger."

We release God's power each time we praise and worship Him. Remember praise exalts Jesus and magnifies Him. It is like turning on the floodlights and dispelling the darkness.

Pray in the Spirit

I want to encourage you that as you pray more in the Spirit, you will be in tune more with the Holy Spirit. Let me explain.

The Holy Spirit is the One who gives the language Acts 2:4 says, "[They] began to speak with other tongues, as the Spirit gave them utterance."

When we are praying in the Spirit we are giving the Holy Spirit a place in our life.

Interpretation of tongues is also from the Holy Spirit (1 Cor. 12:10). Paul said we can pray for our tongues to be interpreted. He adds, "I will pray with the spirit, and I will pray with the understanding also: I will sing with the spirit, and I will sing with the understanding also" (1 Cor. 14:15).

You can alternate between praying in the Spirit and praying in English (or your native language). God will give you interpretation to your own prayers, and you will become so sensitive to the Spirit that you hear God saying things to you as though someone picked up a phone and called you.

In the summer of 1992 we were needing more space for our ministry. To build would take us a couple of years with our cash approach. Yet we needed space that very year. One August afternoon I was in my office just wondering what to do. I felt impressed to stop working and pray for a while.

Within ten minutes a thought began to flood my mind and onto my lips as I prayed in tongues. The Spirit spoke to seek buying the former Oral Roberts Evangelistic Association (OREA) building located about half a mile from our building.

The building had been traded to a company months earlier for work that was being done by that company. The building was no longer needed by OREA as they had other space on the ORU campus for its work

I made contact with the owner who told me his company had just decided to sell the building because of a cash flow need. It was about to be publicly advertized for sale within three to four days of my call.

He needed cash immediately and we offered 1.5 million dollars to be paid in 49 days (seven weeks). As I shared the need with our church, the people saw the miracle of buying a 102,000 square foot building on 12.5 acres. To buy that land today and build at fifty dollars per square foot would have cost us well over $6 million. In our way of thinking, it was a $4.5 million gift!

The Holy Spirit knew what to do and revealed it to me through praying in the Spirit and interpretation.

Oh, the joy to hear from God and see Him perform the miracle. In forty-nine days the money came in and Victory paid cash for the land and building that nearly doubled our size in one day. To God be the glory!

There's an important way God leads that I have mentioned several times in this book. It is through visions. In the next chapter I want to help you recognize visions and understand their purpose.

CHAPTER SIXTEEN

THE VISION
OF THE LORD

I like to say the Holy Spirit is in charge of God's audio-visual department. Several times in my life the Lord has used visions to guide me. Sometimes those visions are actual pictures that are seen. Other times they are words that are heard through our spirits.

As I said before, a vision is not a merit badge or a sign of great approval from God. Visions are often the way He tells us something we need to know.

The prophet Joel spoke that in the last days God

would pour out His Spirit on everyone: men and women, young and old (Joel 2:28). Everyone would have an opportunity for the outpouring of the Holy Spirit.

What is a vision from the Lord? How does it come? What is the purpose? It's all in the Scriptures. I want to give you seven reasons for visions.

Reasons for Visions

1. God gives visions to make His will known.

Amos 3:7 says God will do nothing except He reveals it to His servants the prophets.

Numbers 12:6 says that if God wants to make Himself known, He can reveal Himself in a vision.

When I was eighteen years old, I had a vision of Sharon ministering with me as my wife. That vision was an open vision, something I saw as if it were on a video screen. God wanted me to know His will about who to marry. I don't think everybody has to have that kind of vision, but for some reason God thought I needed it.

It was more than three years and three months from the time of that vision until we were married. Perhaps that's what we needed to carry us through all those years of dating.

God also makes His will known through a vision shared by a leader. God's vision can come to one individual and be imparted to a multitude of people. That vision then becomes your vision if you're hooked up to it and latch your faith to it.

2. *God gives a vision so you can be prepared for the future.*

Habakkuk 2:2 says, "And the Lord answered me, and said, Write the vision, and make it plain upon tables, that he may run that readeth it."

There's a time when the vision comes to pass that you're going to need to run with it. Through the vision, the Lord is preparing you to be able to act when the time is right. In the early 1980s I had thoughts of preaching in Russia to help bring in the harvest of the lost. Before the door ever opened God was preparing my heart for the work that would come.

3. *God gives a vision to warn others.*

Not every vision comes for the purpose of warning others, but some do. Nahum had a vision about Nineveh being destroyed (Nah. 3:7). Jeremiah and Ezekiel had visions causing them to warn others. Noah had a vision of coming judgment, and he warned people, even though they didn't pay attention.

In 1980 we had several prophets warn our church to get out of debt. They warned that financial woes were coming to America, reversals, difficult times. I wish I had heeded that vision at the time. I heard it, but I didn't commit to it. I didn't understand then it was possible to get out of debt.

In 1981 the church took out a loan for the auto mart with a floating interest rate. Interest rates floated way up and we experienced the pain and difficulty of tremendous debt at 15 percent interest. I learned a lesson the hard way. Listen to the warning that comes from the prophets of God.

In 1982 we made a decision to get out of debt

and operate on a cash basis. It happened in 1985. From that date until now we have not borrowed, but have believed God for the funds to pay as we go. The land and buildings we now own were all purchased with cash, and the ministry is debt-free. The result is the blessing God promised when He first spoke to us. Thank God for His mercy.

4. God gives a vision so you can cooperate with Him.

Paul stood before King Agrippa and said, "I was not disobedient unto the heavenly vision" (Acts 26:19).

What was Paul's vision? God stopped him on his way to persecute Christians in Damascus and told him his life had another purpose: "I have appeared unto thee for this purpose, to make thee a minister and a witness both of these things which thou hast seen, and of those things in the which I will appear unto thee" (Acts 26:16).

God gave Paul a vision so he could cooperate with Him and follow God's plan for his life. Paul had to make some adjustments, but by the time he got to King Agrippa he could say he had not been disobedient to the vision.

In the summer of 1994, T. L. and Daisy Osborn asked to meet with Sharon and me to share something that was on their hearts. The Osborns had preached mass miracle crusades in other countries since the 1940s. They had built a ministry headquarters building with over 108,000 square feet of floor space. There were offices, auditoriums and large storage areas in the building. But they were no longer using it because of changes in their ministry.

On the morning we were to meet with them, I felt impressed to ask the Lord what they were going to say. Immediately it came to my spirit that they were going to talk to us about their building. My mind dismissed it, thinking we would not want to buy a building three miles from our other locations.

As they talked with us that afternoon, they didn't ask us to *buy* the building. They offered to *give* it to Victory Christian Center for the Victory Bible Institute and the World Missions Training Center. The building, located right on Interstate 44, is highly visible with more than one hundred thousand cars a day passing it. Besides needing some roof repair and new carpet, the building was ready for us to move into immediately.

As the Osborns talked, both Sharon and I had the inner witness of the Holy Spirit that this was God's direction. A joy flooded our beings as we realized the replacement value of the building was several million dollars.

(A later appraisal set the replacement value at $10 million, not counting the land. In other words, if we had to build and equip the building ourselves, we would be facing millions of dollars in costs.)

After three weeks of prayer and seeking God's perfect will, we knew God had planned this miracle. Victory Bible Institute had always been stuck in a small area of each of our buildings since its beginning. It did not have visibility or high priority in our ministry.

But suddenly in the fall of 1994, Victory Bible Institute and the World Missions Training Center had a huge building where they could grow and expand. Putting these ministries in a separate location has given them individual identities and has actually been an advantage rather than a liability

No longer do people view the schools as insignificant programs. Now they can see the value God places on these vital end-time training centers.

As we moved into the facilities, we were like "them that dream" (Ps. 126:1). The main auditorium was completely outfitted the day we moved in with chairs, piano, sound system, flags of countries — all a gift from the Osborns. Huge outlines of the world are on the walls in several areas of the facility. The continents are depicted on the outside walls of the rotunda building to be used for the World Missions Training Center. Hallelujah!

Remember: God's vision depends on your cooperation. We have to align ourselves to the vision God gives us. That means adjustments and changes in our lives.

5. God gives a vision to give you hope in the midst of adverse circumstances.

David said he would have fainted if he had not "believed to see the goodness of the Lord in the land of the living" (Ps. 27:13).

I believe our "blessed hope," which is meeting Jesus in heaven, is a vision that keeps us steadfast in the face of trials (Titus 2:13).

A lot of people have given up on their vision because negative things have happened; persecution or failures have taken place. They put their eyes on people and their own abilities. Keep your eyes on Jesus.

There may be opposition or persecution. Time is short. That's why we have the book of Revelation

— it's a vision to prepare us for the future and help us overcome every work of the enemy.

Joseph's dream carried him through thirteen years of disappointment: being sold into slavery, slandered, thrown in jail and forgotten.

No matter what people do to you, don't get bitter. Instead get better and you'll see the vision come to pass. God will bring it to pass *in due time.*

As you are going toward the vision, many times you'll only be able to see in part. But thank God for every part you see. God's provision will meet you at the end of your full obedience.

When a vision is fulfilled it meets needs right then, but it also inspires people that God can do the same for them. When I hear people talking about their visions and what is coming to pass for them, I don't get jealous. I get inspired with what's happening in their lives. God is not a respecter of persons. He can fulfill His vision in every heart that chooses to believe and obey.

6. God gives a vision to give direction.

Peter saw a vision from heaven, a sheet full of unclean animals (Acts 10). The Lord said, "Kill and eat," and Peter replied, "No, Lord. They're unclean." That happened three times.

The Lord finally told him, "Don't call common or unclean what I have cleansed."

Immediately there came to the door of the house messengers from a man named Cornelius, a Gentile He was a person that Peter would call unclean because he was not Jewish. Peter believed the gospel was only for the Jews. But God was giving him a new direction. God gives supernatural direction by visions and dreams.

Paul had a dream to go to the region of Macedonia. The first city they visited was Philippi (Acts 16). Things started out well there, but they ended up being beaten and thrown in jail. Just because you have a vision doesn't mean there won't be opposition.

What do you do when your vision is attacked? What do you do when you have opposition? You keep on praising God. You keep on magnifying the Lord. That's what Paul and Silas did in jail. The day will come when there is a release and God gives the breakthrough. Paul didn't stay in prison; God sent an earthquake that literally shook them free.

7. *God gives you a vision or dream to keep you from pride.*

When Peter went to speak to Cornelius and his family, the Holy Ghost fell on them. But Peter couldn't boast in it because God had revealed ahead of time that He was going to accept the Gentiles.

You see, when it's from the Lord, you can't boast over what you've done. You can't say your might or power did it. You just have to say, "God did it." He brought it to pass. God gets the glory. He's honored.

> In a dream, in a vision of the night,
> When deep sleep falls upon men,
> While slumbering on their beds,
> Then He opens the ears of men,
> And seals their instruction.
> In order to turn man from his deed,
> And conceal pride from man
> (Job 33:15-17, NKJV).

Responding to a Vision

Remember: A vision from the Lord will be in line with the written Word of God. It will never contradict what the Bible says. Another way to test a vision is to look at the fruit it brings into your life. Does it draw you to seek the Lord and trust in Him?

After you test your vision, you have to decide who to tell. Seek the Lord for direction. Some visions are meant for your personal edification and encouragement and you don't need to share those with everyone.

When I had a vision of our congregation meeting at the Mabee Center, I only told my wife. That way, when the vision came to pass, all the glory went to God, and we knew it was God who did it.

Other visions are meant for you to share and work toward with many other people. Having one million copies of *This Is Your Life* printed in Russian was a vision I shared with my congregation. Many people worked to make those books a reality. But only God could have orchestrated the events in Russia enabling us to distribute those books where the door had been closed.

Having a vision does not mean things will necessarily happen the way you expect them to. I had a vision in the fall of 1974 that I would be the next pastor of Sheridan Christian Center. Do you know the next thing the Holy Spirit told me to do? Leave Sheridan to travel and preach fulltime. Then I got planted in the middle of a campground selling snacks and organizing volleyball.

In the natural, those moves looked like steps in the wrong direction. But that didn't matter in the supernatural. A vision will always require you to do two things: wait and trust. I call it being in the waiting room of the Holy Spirit.

I was in the waiting room for four years with that vision, but when it happened, I knew it was in God's timing. You spend a lot of time in the waiting room when you're led by God's Spirit, but that's where you'll grow. God fulfilled the vision He gave me after He had prepared me to handle it. The waiting room I'm speaking of is not a place of inactivity but a place of intense preparation.

Seeking Visions

You can't do anything that will make the Holy Spirit speak one way or the other. So don't reject other ways the Holy Spirit leads. Don't insist on having a vision where you "see" things. Say, "Father, I am ready and willing to hear Your voice," and He will honor your desire in His perfect way.

Remember the three steps to inviting the Holy Spirit to guide you: 1) desire to hear Him, 2) listen and 3) ask specifically. Accept whatever way He speaks:

- His Word
- words from the Holy Spirit that well up in your spirit
- an inward witness
- a sense of peace
- a lack of peace
- interpretation of your own tongues

141

- divine encounters

- dreams

God is very creative. We would be foolish to demand that He speak to us in a certain way.

If you have a desire to be led by the Spirit of God, I invite you to express that to Him right now. I encourage you to pray this prayer:

> Father, I come to You in the name of Jesus asking to be led by Your Holy Spirit. As I acknowledge You, please direct my steps. Show me things to come. Cause me to hear Your voice. I refuse to listen to other misleading voices. Give me a hearing ear and a discerning heart. Fill me with the knowledge of Your will.

Praise the Lord for what that prayer will start in your life today!

Billy Joe Daugherty pastors Victory Christian Center in Tulsa, Oklahoma, and ministers daily through television and radio. He's the author of numerous books and founder of Victory Christian School, Victory Bible Institute and the World Missions Training Center.

Other books by Billy Joe Daugherty:

Absolute Victory

Building Stronger Marriages and Families

The Demonstration of the Gospel

Faith Power

This New Life

You Can Be Healed

For more information about his ministry or other books, you may contact:

Victory Christian Center
7700 S. Lewis
Tulsa, OK 74136
(918) 493-1700